THE
LITERARY
PERCYS

Family History,

Gender, and the

Southern Imagination

Bertram Wyatt-Brown

Mercer University Lamar Memorial Lectures
No. 37

The University of Georgia Press
ATHENS AND LONDON

© 1994 by the University of Georgia Press
Athens, Georgia 30602
All rights reserved

Designed by Kathi L. Dailey
Set in Linotype Walbaum by Tseng Information Systems, Inc.
Printed and bound by Maple-Vail Book Manufacturing Group
The paper in this book meets the guidelines for
permanence and durability of the Committee on
Production Guidelines for Book Longevity of the
Council on Library Resources.

Printed in the United States of America

98   97   96   95   94   C   5   4   3   2   1

Library of Congress Cataloging in Publication Data

Wyatt-Brown, Bertram, 1932–
The literary Percys : family history, gender, and the Southern
imagination / Bertram Wyatt-Brown.
p. cm. — (Mercer University Lamar memorial lectures ;
no. 37)
Includes bibliographical references (p.) and index.
ISBN 0-8203-1665-2
1. Percy, Walker, 1916–   —Family.   2. American literature—
Southern States—History and criticism.   3. Women and
literature—Southern States—History.   4. Southern States—
Intellectual life.   5. Family—Southern States—History.
6. Southern States—In literature.   7. Authorship—Sex
differences.   8. Percy family.
I. Title.   II. Series.
PS3566.E6912Z98   1994
813' .54—dc20   94-4173

British Library Cataloging in Publication Data available

This book is dedicated to the memory of
Natalie Jewett Marbury
and to Natalie Ingraham Wyatt-Brown
and Susan Fendall Marbury

CONTENTS

PREFACE

The opportunity to present the Eugenia Dorothy Blount Lamar Memorial Lectures in the fall of 1993 at Mercer University in Macon, Georgia, was most welcome. The honor put me in company with such distinguished predecessors as Sam Hill, my colleague at the University of Florida, Louis D. Rubin, Jr., Lewis P. Simpson, Cleanth Brooks, Fred Hobson, and the late Marcus Cunliffe, to name only a few of the lecturers. No less gratifying was the chance to explore an aspect of the Percy family that could not be adequately explored in a larger and more biographical study, *The House of Percy*, just completed and soon to appear with a different press. Although some information and interpretation inevitably must be presented in both works, the lecture series afforded an exposition of the role that gender played in the history of this extraordinary and creative family for over one hundred years.

Lucinda H. MacKethan, in her *Daughters of Time*, the Lamar Lectures that appeared in 1990, set the agenda for further recoveries of a female tradition in Southern letters. In her opening remarks Professor MacKethan of North Carolina State University recalls Edna Earle Ponder, Eudora Welty's nonstop storyteller in *The Ponder Heart*.

Like so many Southern women of Welty's generation, Edna Earle sits in the shadow of a dominating male relative. She seems, explains MacKethan, to occupy the post of a "silent servant." When her Uncle Daniel holds forth in his usual garrulous fashion, his niece slides into the background. By the end of the story, however, we realize that Edna Earle Ponder is the heroine. As MacKethan reminds us, Edna Earle has quietly usurped the storytelling function and even the identity of her now-silent Uncle Daniel.[1]

MacKethan's reference to *The Ponder Heart* has pertinence to the themes explored here. The first two chapters concern three female storytellers who were connected with the Percy family of Mississippi—Eleanor Percy Lee, her sister Catherine Ware Warfield, and Eleanor's daughter, Sarah Catherine (Kate) Lee Ferguson. Their collateral descendants included the male writers William Alexander Percy, author of the classic memoir *Lanterns on the Levee*, and Walker Percy, one of the most respected and profound novelists that the twentieth-century South has produced. Writing out of the same sources of tragedy and depression that later afflicted Will and Walker Percy, these women told their tales but have long since been forgotten, even by family members.

The female literary tradition in the family began in 1843 and then abruptly ceased in 1894, the result of a scandal that ended the career of the last in the line. Even the names of the women themselves disappeared from the storehouse of Percy memories. Will Percy, the family chronicler, mentioned none of them in his celebrated autobiography. Instead he glorified the honorable bearing and virtue of even the most obscure among the Percy males. Women simply did not count in the family annals, a situation in the South hardly peculiar to the Percy clan. And yet by the same mysterious process by which Edna Earle Ponder assumed gradual control, we find that the feminine element re-appeared in the work of Walker Percy in guises of which even he was unaware. By some circumstance that could not be wholly coincidental, one of Walker Percy's novels bore uncanny resemblance to a romance that a kinswoman had published over a hundred years earlier but which neither he nor anyone else in the family had ever heard of, much less read.

These chapters explore the role of gender and a ten-dency to melancholy in this Southern literary family and how these factors affected the literary genres in which the writers expressed themselves. But they also concern the more intangible problem of what might be called literary androgyny, the ability of writers to draw upon the subter-ranean springs of an opposite sexuality in fleshing out their characters.

I am indebted to a number of individuals at Mercer Univer-sity for their warm and generous hospitality. Wayne Mixon originally arranged for my visit and offered a very kind introduction at the third and final lecture. His published work, as the references here will attest, helped to substanti-ate my argument. Michael M. Cass took over the director-ship of the Lamar Series from Wayne, and no speaker could have asked for a more solicitous and efficient impresario, helped, as he was, by his charming wife Lynn. I also thank the members of the Lamar Memorial Lectures Committee, most especially Hubert H. McAlexander, Mrs. R. Lanier Anderson III, and Henry Y. Warnock. The experience of being a guest at Mercer University is quite exhilarating, and the guest is at once struck by the friendliness of the students and the intellectual vitality of the faculty. A visitor also marvels at the handsome architecture on campus and along the surrounding streets where antebellum homes and late Victorian mansions have a stateliness matched by the ancient oaks that shade them.

Many others also deserve my gratitude. At the University of Florida, several graduate assistants—Stan Deaton, Tim Huebner, Daniel Kilbride, and Andrew Frank—checked references and text, read microfilm, or performed other essential tasks with dispatch and goodwill. B. J. Clager, a secretary with uncommon skill and conscientiousness, eased the burdens of a heavy schedule during the time that these pages were being prepared. One could not ask for a more cooperative office staff than that of the Department of History, most notably Betty Corwine.

With heartfelt gratitude I also acknowledge the contribution of Anita Rutman. Although busy helping her husband Darrett put the finishing touches on a book of their essays, Anita applied her unerring editorial judgment to a major problem of length and direction in the writing of *The House of Percy*. The solution that she suggested made possible the fashioning of this series for the Lamar Lectures. Lucas Myers of San Francisco and Otto Olsen of Gainesville put their critical powers to use on early versions of these chapters. Charles East of Baton Rouge saved me from many errors of fact and style.

Institutions and the people connected with them have also made the task of writing easier and more pleasant than it ordinarily is. I began this project as a happy inmate at the National Humanities Center in Research Triangle Park,

North Carolina, 1989–1990. For a week or so in September 1993 Robert Connor and Kent Mullikin amiably allowed me, a hopeless recidivist, to occupy a vacant office where these lectures were shaped. Some years ago the National Endowment for the Humanities granted me a fellowship which permitted the discovery of the Percy story. I must also mention the University of Florida Foundation, which manages the Richard J. Milbauer Endowment for the chair I hold. The funds from that source enabled me to travel to research sites, attend conferences at home and abroad, fund a dedicated and promising set of graduate students, and meet other academic expenses.

Like the Percys, I have been fortunate to know and love enormously talented women who have enlarged my appreciation of their sex's creative potentiality. Without the insight of my wife Anne, whose expertise spans so many humanistic fields from linguistics to gerontology, this book and almost everything else I have written, thought, or done would be much the poorer. In fact, she suggested the topic of "The Literary Percys" to begin with.

I dedicate this work, however, to three other remarkable women: the two Natalies in our family—my daughter Natalie Ingraham Wyatt-Brown, soon to be a lawyer in Minnesota, and my mother-in-law, Natalie Jewett Marbury—and my sister-in-law Susan Fendall Marbury of Baltimore, who cheerfully opens her door to snappish and weary travelers from Florida when they unceremoniously appear. Unfortunately Natalie Jewett Marbury did not live to see this dedication, but none of her children or in-laws will forget her humor, graciousness, and kindness to us over the years.

Chapter One

THE
FIRST PERCY
WRITERS

*No family in America
has a more curious history than the Percys
of Mississippi, and few have had so many gifted members.*
The first chapter and the two to follow will show how this
exceptional lineage contributed to Southern letters. Early
in my researches I discovered that Walker Percy and his
guardian William Alexander Percy, both writers of exceptional depth and imagination, belonged to a clan that
had already demonstrated literary talent in the nineteenth
century.

The female writers Eleanor Percy Lee and Catherine
Ann Warfield, subjects of the first chapter, published two
substantial volumes of poetry and wrote ten novels, nine of
them published. They were sisters, children of Sarah Percy
Ware and her husband Nathaniel Ware. Although not discussed on this occasion, Sarah Anne Ellis Dorsey, the Ware
sisters' niece, produced one first-rate biography of a Confederate leader and five novels. Ellen Lee's daughter, who
will later be treated extensively, published one novel in
1889 before her literary career was permanently ended by
a devastating scandal. It is ironic that these women, with
a total of eighteen works in bound editions, would have
won any "publish or perish" academic contest against their
well-known and better-prepared male successors Will and
Walker Percy, whose total of hardcover works came to
eleven.[1]

Yet there is more at stake in dealing with the Percys
than following their trail of literary glory. Literary schol-
ars and biographers have become ever more aware that
art is not merely a matter of imaginative genius. The liter-

ary craft involves personal and, most particularly, familial experience as well. The historian Joel Williamson has recently uncovered the history of the "black Faulkners," a story of miscegenation that enriches our appreciation for the great novelist's *Absalom, Absalom!* and other fictional works. Lawrence Friedman is now completing a biography of Erik H. Erikson, the renowned psychologist best known for his exploration of the "identity crisis" of young manhood. The basis for the idea was Erikson's own adolescent search for his real father to whom his mother had been neither married nor long attached.[2] The poetry of Sylvia Plath and Anne Sexton must be read in light of what their biographers tell us about their mood swings and suicidal tendencies.[3] Likewise, we will find in the Percy saga not just the roots of Walker Percy's fiction but much more. A study of the Percys concerns the interrelationship of family life and the creative impulse, even when that impulse could only be expressed within the narrow constrictions of popular nineteenth-century romance.

So conventional were the writings of the Percy-related artists—Ellen Lee, Catherine Warfield, Sarah Dorsey, and Kate Ferguson—that they could never have achieved lasting fame. That conventionality was a function of their sex and time. Poverty and workaday drudgery were not the causes for a limited artistic range in middle-class nineteenth-century women's writing. Like so many women writers, they felt themselves "defeminized," as Helen Taylor points out, by "the very act of writing for publication." Some apologized for even venturing into such hazardous waters. Elizabeth Bisland Wetmore, for instance, prefaced her romance *Blue and Gray, Or, Two Oaths and Three Warnings* in this way: "Our mind may not be stored with lore or logic, and far from brilliant, yet we disdain useless pollysyllables [*sic*], aiming but to indite a plain sensible recital."[4]

Like her more submissively domesticated sisters on the plantation, the Southern woman writer also had to struggle with the dominant patriarchal world surrounding her. It was a realm in which writing itself, whether the product of a male or female imagination, was considered a frivolous, unmanly enterprise. The innate conservatism about manners and sexual differentiations that slavery and race subordination demanded was bound to limit the female experience in the larger world and thereby diminish imaginative horizons. The ideal Southern woman, observes Anne Goodwyn Jones, "is chaste because she has never been tempted."[5] Virtue among women was the *absence* of action; it was thought disgraceful for them to do anything in many spheres of life beyond the hearth and marital bedchamber.

Equally significant was the unfocused and undemanding form of education which prepared women, especially Southern women, for the entertainment of men but not for a goal-driven approach to any subject of study, including art. Having women's alleged mental and emotional and even moral inferiority drilled into them even as they learned French or were practicing on the harp, women, like those of Percy descendance, lacked intellectual self-confidence. At a moment of exasperation, novelist Sarah Dorsey, the Ware sisters' niece, replied to a condescending letter from a male intellectual, "*What* must *I* read, what training must I individually go through" to achieve artistic and philosophical excellence? She was prepared, she vowed, to undertake any course of study her friend might recommend. Like other women of mind, she found it hard to understand why her reading of the same books that men read did not train her "as a man is educated by them."[6] They, however, had undergone a purposeful and constructive program at college that led to a sense of professional competence. Women's education lacked that kind of expectation. Later in the nineteenth century, matters had not materially improved. When Ellen Glasgow, the Southern novelist, sought the advice of a New York literary agent, he responded, "You are too pretty to be a novelist. Is your figure as lovely in the altogether as it is in your clothes?" He then tried to rape her.[7]

Equally important was the lack of prior example upon which mid-Victorian women could draw to sustain ambitions. One might argue that there was a tradition from Aphra Behn through Mary Wollstonecraft and Jane Austen, but it was not acknowledged to be a tradition, even by aspiring women writers. Although from one-half to two-thirds of all eighteenth-century novels in English were written by women, no secure heritage developed and hence no models were provided. Without noted exemplars, as literary critic Joanna Russ observes, "It's hard to work; without context, difficult to evaluate; without peers, nearly impossible to speak." The Ware sisters and their niece Sarah Dorsey had each other and a few women friends upon whom to test their literary efforts. Other sources for feminine inspiration did not exist.[8]

The situation for literary women, however, was beginning to change. A female audience had long existed, but it was growing in size as Americans became more prosperous and women more conscious of their separate interests and needs. Yet, despite the growth of the pulp trade in the

Jacksonian era, the trend did not progress without critical disapproval. In 1847, for instance, Emily Brontë published *Wuthering Heights* pseudonymously; it was greeted by the more discerning critics as "bold" and "original." But when her name was attached to it in a second edition in 1850, the novel was at once dismissed as a mirror of "the 'distorted' fancy of the writer's life, which was isolated and deprived." [9] How hard it was to be among the first to grapple with art when such manifold discouragements were thrown in the way.

These remarks almost border on the cliché in these self-consciously feminist times, but *why* the female pioneers defied the obstacles so persistently remains unexamined. Through the prism afforded by the works of these Percy-descended women, one can see how their gender, their personal experience, and the forms of literature they chose—the gothic-sentimental and later the proto-feminist—were so closely connected. They did not write simply to gain commercial rewards; they did so largely out of personal desperation. The circumstances surrounding their creative process tell us much about the limitations confronting female artists but also how they were able to make art out of personal materials at hand, experiences that had their own tragic integrity.

The first two chapters concern the role of these Percy-related women in literary creativity and how their subjects were associated with family history. I omit the work of Sarah Anne Ellis Dorsey, who is examined elsewhere, although her instrumentality in the revival of her aunt Catherine Warfield's literary interests is part of the story to be recounted.[10] The last chapter explores Walker Percy's use of a purely male genre—the mock-heroic—and how it reflected his personal and his familial concerns.

Before proceeding further, something must be said about the peculiar history of the Percy tribe. The story begins with Charles Percy, the founder, a rogue who seems almost to have stepped out of Thackeray's *Barry Lyndon* or De Molinas's *Don Juan*. An Irish foot soldier during the Seven Years' War, Percy claimed to be kin to the noble house of Northumberland, whose most famous member was "Harry Hotspur" Percy, the reckless insurgent of Shakespeare's *Henry IV.* Leaving a woman, to whom he was possibly but not certifiably married, and two children behind in the British Isles, Charles absconded to America in the 1770s. There followed an adventure with a woman of the Bermuda Islands, to whom, again, he might have been married. She died before long, allegedly because discovery of his prior family arrangements had shocked her into insensibility. In his next incarnation, Charles married in 1780 a sixteen-year-old heiress named Susannah Collins.[11]

In 1790, however, a son by the first union turned up to confront his father. Fulfilling the dying wish of his long-deserted mother, Robert Percy, a lieutenant in the Royal Navy, had tracked father Charles down to his plantation on the present border between Louisiana and Mississippi. Some years later, during an episode of depression with psychotic symptoms, Charles committed suicide by leaping into a Mississippi River tributary with an iron pot roped to his neck. The widow Susannah reared the couple's children successfully. Under her management Charles's estate of land, slaves, crops, and cattle grew to a value of nearly $50,000, a sum equivalent to a half million or more today.[12]

At the turn of the nineteenth century Robert, the sole legitimate heir, left the navy and settled himself in the same vicinity, not far from Natchez, Mississippi. Thus, two Percy families continued to thrive within easy distance of each other in Mississippi and in Louisiana. All of the literary Percys, including Walker, were descendants of the Susannah Collins line. Yet the existence of rivals, possibly with purer bloodlines, so close by may help to explain why mythmaking and fiction writing were the stock-in-trade of these proud folk. What could not be demonstrated in fact could at least be imagined and assumed.

The next generation was no luckier than the first, with significant consequences for its members and those that followed. Charles Percy's eldest daughter Sarah was ten in 1794 when her father plunged to his death in the black waters of Buffalo Creek, thereafter called Percy Creek. No one could have guessed that the fatality would affect her later life. Yet at that age daughters become most attached to their fathers, and a loss of this kind could have had serious repercussions that might not appear for many years. So it was in this case. In 1819, when she was thirty-nine years old, immediately upon the birth of her second daughter of a second marriage, Sarah lost her reason in an extreme form of post-partum depression. Following her father's madness, she was the second victim to what would prove to be a persistent and unpredictable problem of chronic depression for the family over the next 150 years.

Sarah's husband, a dour and mercurial financier and explorer named Nathaniel Ware, left Mississippi and established himself, his wife, and two infants in Philadelphia. In that distant city Sarah could be housed and treated at the Pennsylvania Hospital, virtually the only institu-

tion in America that handled mentally disturbed patients
in a clinical way. Major Ware grew ever more reclusive
as a result of his unhappy situation—unable to remarry
but separated by mental illness from the companionship of
a wife. He tried to compensate for his unenviable situation by extensive travels, interest in the natural sciences,
especially soil chemistry and botany, and acquisition of a
large library devoted to scientific subjects, the writings of
agnostics like Voltaire, and romantic literature.

Formidable and gloomy, Ware almost mesmerized his
daughters, and they were bound to make him the object of
much of their fiction and poetry. He even looked the part of
a Byronic intellectual. Conceited about his appearance—
pale complexion, small mouth, tightly pressed, and nose
that a Roman proconsul would have worn with pride—
he was always dressed in the most expensive broadcloth
and silk waistcoat. The Major had once entertained hopes
for a grand political future; he served briefly as acting
governor of the Territory of Mississippi during the first
Monroe Administration. When he ran for popular office,
however, his haughty manners and contempt for the ordinary processes of democracy handed him a humiliating
defeat. Thereafter he sought only appointive posts. Except
for serving briefly as a federal land commissioner, 1821–
1822, in East Florida, newly acquired from Spain, he was
largely rebuffed. Even the high-toned Whigs gave him no
office during the Harrison-Tyler period, although he had
written a tract on political economy in support of Henry
Clay's nationalistic "American Plan." [13] Making use of their
father's image in their imaginative work, the daughters
often wrote of figures who achieved high place in national

affairs but eventually found the pursuit of power an empty and thankless enterprise.

The two children of Sarah and Nathaniel Ware, Catherine Ann and her younger sister Eleanor, whose birth had been the occasion of her mother's insanity, were the first writers to appear in the Percy clan. The controlling experience for them both was a dual problem—the paralyzing melancholy of their mother and the gloom and peculiarity of their father. No doubt their productivity reflected the lack of psychological closure that their mother's illness occasioned. From an emotional point of view she had died and left them upon Ellen's birth, but physically, of course, she was still on earth to be nursed, guarded, and visited. As if a tension between life and death or presence and absence of a loved one stimulated the creative impulse beginning at a very early age, that kind of confusion and irresolution has often been characteristic of an artist's life long after the disruptions occurred.[14]

Nathaniel Ware's situation also affected the young women. "His domestic trials," a reporter later wrote, "rendered him bitter and outwardly morose, even to his friends, sometimes even to his children." He frequently left them in the hands of servants and a forbidding English governess who was apparently replaced later by a Scottish nurse named Janet. Although strict with the children, Janet taught them to sing old Scottish and English folk songs. Meanwhile, he scoured the Southern wilderness looking for profitable tracts to buy and sell.[15]

Sarah Percy Ware's loss of reason and Nathaniel Ware's absenteeism affected the Ware sisters in different ways. Catherine, being the older, felt so abandoned and insecure that she refused to attend school, a not uncommon reaction for a small child under such circumstances. No doubt she feared that unless she stayed home her father would disappear, leaving her an orphan. (Not surprisingly the heroine of her first novel was a young orphan.) The Ware children were attending Madame Sigoigne's French Academy in the Philadelphia suburb of Frankford. One day, however, Catherine escaped from the school and refused to come out of her hiding place in a "wood-closet" belonging to her half sister Mary Jane Ellis LaRoche. Her father and Madame Sigoigne had to promise never to send her back. Thereafter the shy but brilliant pupil was taught at home by tutors and by Major Ware himself.[16]

Visiting their mother heightened the daughters' anxieties. In the 1820s, as if strolling through a zoo, curious onlookers paid a small sum to watch from above as the Pennsylvania Hospital inmates took the air in the dry moat that surrounded the building. Doubtless, Sarah Ware's wealth spared her and her children that humiliation, but Sarah was so chronically demented that she had to have been frightening to her children. The girls' mother would open a book but not read, or she would strum a few "discordant notes" on a beribboned guitar that she once had skillfully played. In her madness, Sarah Percy Ware liked to paint or draw flowers and birds on the walls, yet she would never use pen or brush on canvas or sketching pad. Apparently she retained much of her original beauty, with her abundant hair and delicate features. Yet the contrast between outward appearance and inner disorder was itself a cause for perplexity and sense of unpredictability. Only an exercise of the imagination could make things safer and more orderly.

———

For Sarah Ware, glimmers of reality were all too few; she mostly lived in an empty world apart. Day after day the distracted matron wailed for her husband, feeling, justly, that he had abandoned her. Many years later Sarah Dorsey, her granddaughter, remarked that there was "one never-ceasing cry from her lips after her husband." But Nathaniel Ware, who seldom mentioned her in his correspondence, stayed away as much as possible, unable to hide his shame and contempt for her condition. When he did come to see her, she failed to recognize him.[17]

Ware's reaction was bound to mystify the girls. But worst of all, Sarah Ware "would weep sometimes for her baby 'Ellen,' but would repulse the caresses of the weeping daughter" herself, who in later years would vainly try to explain to her mother "who she was."[18] Naturally self-centered, children are ill-equipped to handle what Wordsworth in "Michael" called "the impotence of grief." The child blames himself or herself for the death or disappearance of the parent, but at the same time resents the parent for an apparent desertion.[19]

Under these circumstances, the Ware sisters' only maternal resource was their half sister Mary Jane LaRoche, Sarah Percy Ware's eldest daughter by her first marriage and the wife of René LaRoche, a Philadelphia doctor. Unfortunately, when the two sisters were in their teens, Mary Jane also lost her reason, probably under conditions similar to Sarah Percy: postpartum depression after the birth of her son Percy LaRoche.[20]

Before that misfortune befell the hapless LaRoches, Major Ware in 1831 moved himself and his daughters to Cincinnati, a more convenient site for traveling down the Mississippi in his restless search for new lands in the South-west. He removed his wife from the Pennsylvania Hospital and settled her in the second-floor rooms of Woodlawn, the Mississippi plantation home of Thomas George Ellis. The planter was Sarah's eldest son by her first marriage to Judge John Ellis of Natchez. Thomas was the brother of the later melancholic Mary Jane.

During the 1830s the sisters visited their mother every summer at the Ellis plantations, and there their poetic interests developed. At age eleven Ellen had already composed her first poem, and like all her other verses throughout her life the sonnet struck a very doleful note. She kept a "Commonplace Book," copying poems that appeared in the newspapers or noting favorite passages from William Cullen Bryant, then a favorite poet and best known for his mordant "Thanatopsis." [21] Although the evidence is circumstantial, further inspiration doubtless came from Eliza DuPuy, a well-born Virginian then serving as governess for Sarah Ellis, the Ware sisters' little niece, at Woodlawn and at Richmond, the Ellis's elegant townhouse in Natchez.[22] A contributor to *Godey's* and other established women's magazines, DuPuy was among the earliest Southern professional female writers, being the author of twenty-five novels. Under her guidance, Ellen wrote a novella called *Agatha*. A reading of the manuscript reveals little maturity but much ambition and liveliness. The plot concerns a plantation girl who has lost her mother and after some predictable but scarcely threatening misfortunes eventually marries her handsome suitor.

With DuPuy's counsel, Ellen and Catherine concentrated chiefly on mastering versification, all in the sentimental fashion of the day. The sisters managed to collaborate on literary projects, but throughout their lives rivalry and interdependence were ambiguously mingled. Ellen was the handsomer and more outgoing of the pair, Catherine the more thoughtful. As the younger sister, Ellen was determined to win her place in the sun, and periodically they broke off communication in angry recriminations. On one occasion, a slave child once owned by Major Ware became the object of their rivalry. In 1849 another dispute arose, although in the few surviving materials its cause was not disclosed. Usually Ellen apologized, recognizing her own willfulness and mollifying her sister by calling her "the leading Star" in composing verse.[23]

Their first volume, titled *The Wife of Leon*, appeared in 1843. The poems were not memorable, although the sales were favorable enough to require a second edition in 1845. According to the preface, the sisters began their writing without intending to inflict their rhymes upon the world. Major Ware, "a parent," the preface declared, "to whom they could refuse nothing," however, had insisted upon their dissemination, and the authors acquiesced with a modesty expected of aspiring female writers. Ware had always been a father solicitous of their artistic development despite his formidable manners and impenetrability.[24]

In the female poetry of the age, springs always gush, forests are ever deep or trackless, vigils always cheerless. "Why" was never used when "wherefore" could replace it; "wert" was thought more poetic than a simple "were." "Gloom" generally rhymed with "tomb," unless "loom," "doom," or "room" better fit the meaning. The sisters faithfully obeyed these artistic formulations. Yet at least the female Percys' earliest verses rose a little above the level of Emmeline Grangerford's "Ode to Stephen Dowling Bots, Dec'd," in Twain's *Huckleberry Finn*.[25]

Unfortunately echoes of other poets added little to the freshness of the lines. "The Deserted House" has a Bryant-like morbidity; another poem imitated Tennyson's "Lady of Shallot" with hints of Coleridge and Wordsworth here and there.[26] But the circumstances that called forth this kind of effort are worth pursuing. They help to explain the feminine desire for self-expression, no matter how unsophisticated, trite, and derivative the result might have been. Quite understandably, women like Warfield and Lee have long been subjected to harsh criticism—almost all of it by males. Nathaniel Hawthorne's complaint, echoed by countless observers from that day to the recent past, bears repeating: "America is now wholly given over to a damned mob of scribbling women, and I should have no chance of success while the public taste is occupied with their trash."[27] Mary Kelley, a more recent critic, rejoins by calling the kind of writer that the Ware sisters represent "*literary domestics*" rather than mere "sentimentalists."[28] What Kelley and other observers sometimes fail to recognize is that the creative impulse had its origin in pain—or so it was in this instance.

One of the more revealing and successful of the sisters' poems in *The Wife of Leon* was called "I Have Seen This Place Before." The poets were concerned with what Walker Percy would later refer to in *The Last Gentleman* as déjà vu—the snatches of terrifying memory that link past and present. In the fashion of the day, Warfield and Lee identified the sense of repeated experience with the notion of reincarnation. Upper-class women of the mid-Victorian era were often intrigued with the idea of the human spirit returning to earth in a new body. Sarah Dorsey, Lee and

Warfield's niece, would later study Sanskrit in order better to appreciate what she called the "Aryan philosophy" of the Hindus. "I Have Seen This Place Before," however, does not merely refer to the Eastern concept of spiritual regeneration. Instead, the poem suggests that Warfield and Lee's "meditative fancy," as a contemporary critic declared, had a "mysterious" character that involved depression, decay, and death rather than reincarnated vitality.

> In a dream, a midnight dream,
> I have stood upon this heath,
> With this blue and winding stream,
> And the lonely vale beneath;
> The same dark sky was there,
> With its bleak shade on my brow,
> The same deep feeling of despair
> That clings about me now.[29]

The poem was the only one in the volume that suggested the possibilities of future poetic growth.

Having made their debut as the "Two Sisters of the West" on the title page of *The Wife of Leon*, they issued a second volume called *The Indian Chamber*. The subjects remained very much in the gothic and sentimental mode. There were more farewells to loved ones around whom "shadows of the grave" were "falling."[30] Nevertheless, the poems, though still uneven and rhythmically dubious, revealed intellectual maturing and sometimes convincing passion. The authors were beginning to develop a self-confidence that permitted an exploration of their deeper feelings. "The Natchez Lighthouse," for instance, centered upon the death of Sarah Percy Ware, the sisters' mother, that event having occurred in 1836. In another poem, "A Tale of Life," they dealt with Sarah Percy Ware's insanity. Her children "clung in gladness round her knee" but she could only "look up to heaven abstractedly" and move her lips "as if she spoke to one no more on earth." The poets make it seem that the children's mother was mentally broken because of her husband's wild behavior on his trips far from her, so that he "died a death of sin and wo[e], forsaken and alone."[31]

Catherine and Eleanor were too timid and inexperienced to deal directly with their mother's rejection of them; they preferred to treat her as a victim of neglect rather than see themselves in that light. After all, these were the poems of "an innocent and joyous childhood," as Catherine Warfield later wrote her niece Kate Ferguson, Ellen's daughter. There was precious little joy to be detected in the verses, but she meant the joy of creativity, not of subject matter.[32] Instead, the young poets mourned Sarah Ware's death with lines like "Oh, *mother!* do I hear thy voice / Amid the woods of pine?" The poets' mother answers that she can be detected in "nature's wild wind minstrelsy" that peoples "the pathless wilderness / With vanished things again!"[33]

The sisters also began to treat their relationship to their father in a more direct way than they had earlier. Major Ware had himself shown some literary pretensions beyond the writing of botanical papers for the American Philosophical Society of which he was a member. A romantic as well as a scientist, in 1848 he published a stiff and dullish adventure story called *Henry Belden*, which was probably based on his travels in North Africa. Ware's daughters both worshiped and dreaded him, and in the absence of their mother he dominated their lives even after both had married. At some level, though, they felt a deep alienation. The theme appears in "They Tell Me There's an Eastern Bird:"

> And thou art like that God-struck man,
> Forever wandering on;
> Thy spirit's doom is weird and wan;
> Alone! Alone! Alone! [34]

Another set of stanzas is less censorious and more pleading, urging the often absent parent to remain in "our Eden home." "Wander no more dear Father!" they warn, since "*ambition* is a phantom fleeing / A shadow and a dream." [35]

In a sense the daughters thought Major Ware had been partially responsible for their mother's illness. Entitled "Remorse," one poem, however, slides away from such considerations to study the abstraction of depression rather than its devastating intensity. In any event, the poets tell of a man who has greedily acquired national power but who in his later years regrets past misdeeds and plummets toward despair with thoughts of suicide. The poetic figure longs for "*the waters of oblivion*" and admits to his precious wife that life with him has always been difficult because of his tendency to "gloomy mood," "sad fantastic humor," and "wild dream / Whose mutterings startled thee from midnight sleep / To fearful watches." [36] Remorse comes like a beast at twilight bringing, the poets say, "dearth, and restlessness, and agony." The wife seeks to comfort her husband, but in vain. Yet he feels that somehow his melancholy has aroused the genius in him even as it was destroying his peace of mind.

> A sickness and a weariness have crept
> Of late across my spirit, and a vague

And dreamy craving for *reality*—
For all things seem like shadows. Men move by
As forms we dimly see in midnight dreams;
And the vast crowd, with all its upcast heads,
Seems often a phantasma to my eyes.
All but the sense of one great agony,
And that is like the sea—unslumbering;
And that is like the stars—unchangeable. . . .[37]

This stark description of the depressive mentality was among the first of many in the family's literary saga stretching all the way to Walker Percy. It may have been occasioned by the death of the poets' half sister Mary Jane Ellis LaRoche. Still subject to her depressive condition, she had died in 1844 from consumption. Eleanor Percy Lee had been most distressed when Mary Jane had lost her reason in 1838, an event, declared a friend, "from which Ellen never recovered." As a memorial to the once intellectually lively Mary Jane, Ellen wrote her most impassioned poem, explaining: "When my mother waned away, / Into her dark, unbroken rest, / "And I a tiny infant lay, *Thou* camest, and took'st me to thy breast."[38]

In a similar and later poem dedicated to their older half sister, Catherine Warfield touched on the topic with even more precision and intensity. She referred directly to Mary Jane's struggle with a mental derangement "too wild, too dark for the soul within." Even if the poet could recall her from death, "again to traverse thy path of woes," she would "forbear—for thy precious sake—and with tears most bitter—forbid thee to wake."[39] Catherine also recognized the terrors of melancholy in herself and in her demented mother, in the restless, morose, and cold-mannered father, in the family stories about Charles Percy's paranoic seizures, and in the "eclipse of reason" that had afflicted Mary Jane LaRoche.[40]

Like most women writers of their day, the sisters found themselves fully immersed in marital life. Eleanor had married a bluff Virginia planter named William Henry Lee, and they settled in Hinds County, Mississippi, on a large plantation that Major Ware had given his daughter as her dowry. He kept a vigilant eye on the young couple's finances.[41] Marital duty and the succession of pregnancies, which the sisters brought to term, were bound to interfere with their literary avocation. According to sister Catherine, Ellen never wrote another poem after her marriage, but one suspects that their literary collaborations in prose continued well into the 1840s. Ellen's first child, Henry Percy Lee, was born prematurely at seven months and nearly died from an infection contracted when the umbilical cord was cut. Always high-strung, Ellen was so attached to the tiny, struggling infant that she confessed to Catherine she fell into hysterical fits of sobbing. Ellen feared she, too, might lose her reason. Moreover, she was too distraught to nurse the baby. A "rough neighbor" told her husband, " '*Damn it, Lee, the child's starved.*' " Ellen's husband promptly found a black wet nurse, and the baby survived.[42]

At age seventeen in 1833 Catherine had also chosen a country squire for a husband, Elisha Warfield of Lexington, Kentucky, whose father was a prominent medical professor at Transylvania University. Elisha, Jr., was mostly interested in breeding racehorses on the Blue Grass of Lexington, the Warfield family's traditional pastime. (Man o' War was a descendant of a Warfield stud.)

Neither Elisha Warfield nor Harry Lee was intellectually inclined, a circumstance which had the advantage of relieving the sisters of critical remarks about their literary productions. Often enough in the nineteenth century, male artists appropriated their wives' work or refused them permission to practice the craft if it might prove competitive. Gustav Mahler forbade his musically talented wife Alma from composing. (No wonder she had such a vigorous sex life.) The songs of Mendelssohn's sister were credited to her brother, and rumors often attributed the fiction of women writers to their husbands.[43] None of the Percy-descended writers had to face that type of humiliation and misappropriation.

In 1849 Ellen Lee died in a yellow fever epidemic that ravaged Natchez and other parts of the state. Not long before her death she had complained to her husband of being "low-spirited." Also she had been quarreling with Catherine, and the contest of wills did not apparently strengthen her against the disease.[44] The blow was devastating to her sister, as Ellen herself knew it would be. Sarah Anne Ellis, the demented Sarah Ware's grandchild, was at her Aunt Ellen's bedside in Natchez. Sarah Ellis had always promised Aunt Catherine, still living in Lexington, to let her know if her sister Ellen's health were ever endangered. Reminded of the promise, Ellen, dying, turned to her niece and declared, "Oh, what a blow for Catherine!"[45] Indeed, it was. Love, sense of loss, and guilt for surviving mingled in Catherine's bereavement.

In a way rather common among artists with melancholy

---

dispositions, Catherine Warfield reacted to death by ceasing her literary career and falling into a deep despair. She had lost her mother and half sister to insanity and death. As a seeming reinforcement of these earlier losses, Ellen's sudden demise when she was only thirty years old came as a devastating blow, only to be followed in 1853 by the loss of her father. Major Ware succumbed to yellow fever at Galveston, Texas, where he had bought extensive town and country properties. Two events helped to bring Catherine out of her gloom. First, in 1857, Elisha Warfield had suffered financial reverses in the Panic of that year. The family moved to a plantation, which the Warfields called Beechmoor, in the Pee Wee Valley near Louisville.[46] Writing for profit was therefore a motive. Second, upon the insistence of the young niece during a visit from Natchez to Kentucky, Sarah Ellis and her aunt went through the stacks of stories, poems, and half-completed novels in the writing of which the Ware sisters had cooperated years before. Sarah considered it a matter of duty for her aunt to continue the literary tradition which the sisters had begun. But Catherine may not have required much encouragement. She already had a sense of unfinished business. Although she and Ellen had written their poems to express their moods about familial losses and sense of solitude and emotional deprivation, prose fiction would be Catherine's chief means for doing so. "She never sits down to *manufacture* a book," a reporter shrewdly observed later in her career, "she writes because she *must*."[47]

The result of Catherine Warfield's renewed labors was a remarkable gothic tale in two volumes entitled *The Household of Bouverie, Or, the Elixir of Gold*, the first of many prose works from a Percy hand. Catherine Sinclair's 1851

---

best-seller *Jane Bouverie, Or, Prosperity and Adversity*, written in the *Jane Eyre* tradition, was the source of the name. Such shameless borrowing was scarcely uncommon in the growing romance-writing industry.[48] Warfield's tale sold exceedingly well; like all such feminine stories, the work was most successful with the upper-middle-class women of the day for whom it was intended. One Mississippi plantation lady had the nearly eight hundred pages read to her aloud.[49]

According to a contemporary admirer, the novel was "a large-brained book . . . a bold, sharp, live, magnetic creation." Another critic judged it "one of the most striking novels ever written in the South."[50] By this time a few critics were willing to accept novels with cruel, self-absorbed masculine protagonists like Emily Brontë's Heathcliff, but others considered gothic tales much too foreboding for a woman to write. Yet delving into the irrational and violent had become already characteristic of the romances of that day. Earlier, the lengthy and relatively expensive historical romances in the Scott and Cooper mode had given way to cheap novellas in the depression years of the late 1830s and 1840s. By the mid-1850s, when Warfield was writing *The Household of Bouverie*, two-volume fiction, gothic violence, and heavy overlays of Masonic symbolism (this was the age of college fraternity–founding) were all much in vogue. Warfield's work easily found a publisher: Derby and Jackson of New York City, a leader in the pulp trade for romances.

When *The Household of Bouverie* reached the marketplace in 1860, war clouds were swiftly gathering. Other Southern women writers such as Caroline Hentz, Caroline Gilman, and Maria McIntosh had long been glorifying Southern rural life and the supposed benefactions of slavery.[51] Although deeply conservative and herself a slaveowner, Catherine Warfield in her first novel did not rhapsodize over the goodness of planters and the loyalty of slaves, although such matters were casually mentioned here and there. In fact, the servants at the Bouverie mansion are white, and no slave characters materialize at all. The reader is not apprised of what was grown on the Bouverie property, or who grew it. Clearly the author did not wish to be classified as a plantation novelist with a polemical anti–*Uncle Tom's Cabin* agenda. Catherine Warfield was a Whig who, like all others in the Percy-Warfield-Ellis-Ware interconnection, stoutly opposed disunion and thought the "ultras" on both sides to be traitors to civilization and good manners. Yet in common with her kinspeople she became a fanatically loyal Confederate once the decision had been made.[52] In *The Household of Bouverie*, however, Warfield omitted any preaching on the sectional crisis, the sins of abolitionists, and the divinely inspired morality of slaveholders, not because these sentiments struck her as mawkish or inappropriate but because she wished the reader to concentrate on the interior problems of her fictional characters and to read the book as one written by an English storyteller for a transatlantic audience.

An English, even Tory approach in American belles lettres was not at all unusual before the Civil War. Warfield aspired to gratify American female Anglophiles who relished in their fantasies anything steeped in the high-toned customs of the English gentry. As a result, much information is given about the heroine's rearing at Torrington Castle in the north of England, the foreign journeys of other characters, and the peasant ways of the Bouverie ser-

vants, as if they still labored on a feudal estate, touching
their forelocks and chasing off poachers. A sense of place
in America is almost wholly absent. Like Walker Percy
many years later, Warfield liked to consider herself more
European than American in her intellectual interests, but
unlike him, she had no skill in endowing her settings with
much particularity. Given the overtly moral thrust of the
sentimental novel, that type of verisimilitude was not then
highly prized.[53]

To a degree she won praise for her elevated tone and
English orientation. A contemporary writer declared, "Of
living female authors, we can openly class Mrs. Warfield
with George Sand and George Eliot," and her noble sentiments were praised as "Shakespearean." The only American who could match her, said this writer, was Hawthorne.[54]
One could even imagine *The Household of Bouverie* performed as an Italian-style opera with its lavish romanticism
and gothic stage props of octagonal rooms or runic deco-
rations that made the plantation house more a Rosicrucian
temple than a slaveholder's dwelling.

Ambitious in scope though it was, the novel retains
interest less for aesthetic reasons than for two others: its
relationship to the family saga and, because of that connection, its similarity to Walker Percy's novel *Lancelot*, about
which more will be forthcoming.

The heroine is named Lilian de Courcy, another popular
literary designation as the patronym identifies a high-born
family in Anthony Trollope's *Doctor Thorne* and *Framley
Parsonage*. Probably the orphan Lilian, still in her prepu-
bescent years, was meant to be an idealized Ellen Lee.
Henry James once claimed to weary of those motherless
and "precocious little girls" who populated so many senti-

mental novels of that era.[55] But, whether Warfield intended it or not, Lilian was almost a perfect stereotype to explore father-daughter relations, with little attempt at creating a developed figure. Lilian comes from the gloom of Torrington Castle to live in America with her grandmother, Camilla Bouverie, and her collection of eccentric retainers who all reside in an isolated sector of a border slave state. Although she has little of the rebelliousness of Charlotte Brontë's Jane Eyre, Lilian shows enough vigor and curiosity to discover that Erastus Bouverie, her grandfather, long supposed dead, is secretly living on the second floor (site of Warfield's mother's habitat).[56] No visible access exists, but only a secret entry. The original stairs had been removed after Bouverie's alleged demise.

Warfield drew upon the family tales of Charles Percy's peculiarities as the family's first intellectual, but no less important as a model was her own father's record of depression, scientific interests, and wanderlust in the creation of her Faustian antihero Erastus Bouverie. He is a solitary, jealous, and half-mad alchemist in pursuit of a youth-restoring potion. Like other gothic villains and like the real-life depressives whom they often represent, Bouverie could not love nor even tolerate intimacy that might expose his sense of his own self-disgust. Warfield was psychologically acute in attributing his problem to his own upbringing. Bouverie was an orphan reared by a cruel uncle named Ursus (the Bear), a trader in African slaves. His guardian had so undermined his ward's sense of selfhood that he had ever after led a life of repressed fury and undirected grief. Unable to control himself, he must control others by means of duplicity and physical coercion.

Epitomizing this theme is the unholy possessiveness that

Bouverie entertains for his granddaughter. In the course of the plot, he insists upon mixing Lilian's blood with melted sovereigns to produce his life-restoring elixir of gold. The gothic story was the nineteenth-century readers' means of gratifying subliminally inexpressible desires about sex and fears of distorted domestic relations in an acceptable mode. To drink a young woman's blood in a scientist's vial—or more ominously by fanged teeth at the throat, vampire-fashion—was, of course, a literary representation of demonic rape at a time when such abominations could not be graphically presented. In this case, the rape involves incest as well. Bouverie secretly returns from Ulyssean adventures abroad to find that his wife Camilla has presumed him long since dead and has remarried. On the very day of the wedding, like the warrior of Ithaca, he vengefully kills his wife's new lover. As a result he has had to spirit himself out of sight to escape the law, and Camilla, faithful in all things, has for years thereafter seen to his needs and safety, thanks to an unyielding sense of marital loyalty.

In keeping with its English character, the inspiration for the plot came in part from Brontë's *Jane Eyre*. In the Warfield novel, however, the madwoman in the attic is replaced by an equally violent and irrational grandfather. Moreover, just as Rochester's hidden wife Bertha Antoinette in crazed fury bites her brother Richard Mason on the chest to suck the blood and "drain" his very heart, so too Erastus Bouverie tries to show his power in using Lilian's blood in his preparations.[57] In portraying the violence of these figures, the authors sought to put into melodramatic form the problem of insanity and its hideous effect upon the sane—something with which Warfield had personal knowledge. Neither Brontë's Rochester nor Warfield's Camilla Bouverie had any means of escape from the burden of their marriages.

In his own life, as his daughter knew, Major Ware had found that very situation embittering and enslaving. In their reading of *Jane Eyre*, Sandra Gilbert and Susan Gubar have underestimated the peril that Victorians dreaded: marriage to a partner who might be the very opposite of outward appearance—mad, despicable, weak, or roguish. Brontë dealt with the issue from the perspective of the male victim, Warfield from that of an abused but also resentful wife, no less honorable, no less bound to duty than was Brontë's Rochester. The two women shared similarities of familial tragedy. Charlotte Brontë was the motherless daughter of a poor clergyman who lived, said one of her closest friends, "in a walking nightmare of poverty and self-suppression."[58] All her life Catherine Ann Warfield was rich and well favored. Yet both, with siblings sharing their intellectual interests and talents, were dealing with issues of which they all had personal, immediate knowledge, not just fancies drawn solely from the ample treasury of romantic tales then current in the transatlantic canon.

As if cursing her dead father, Catherine Warfield portrayed Bouverie, based on his habits of minds, as the antithesis of a knight-errant. He is a querulous patriarch cowering in his hideaway in the upper galleries, completely dependent upon the reluctant loyalty of a wife whose love for him had disappeared years before. The novel was an attempt to assess how far a woman's loyalty to family and husband should go when surrounded by madness and even violence. Bouverie, the reader eventually learns, has murdered not one but two of his wife Camilla's former suitors, poisoned her canary and her pet dog, spirited away their baby daughter (Lilian's mother) to England and staged a false funeral to deceive his wife, and rendered Camilla's later adopted two-year-old boy Jason mute with jolts of electricity from a galvanic battery.

In addition, Bouverie decides to appropriate his wife's most valuable jewel, a gift from himself, in order to continue his experiments with the elixir. Rather than demand it, he chloroforms her, and the dosage renders her temporarily blind. Then he attaches to her head the electrodes from his infamous galvanic battery and jars her into insensibility. Lilian arouses her, and the victim recalls, "I saw him bending over me with his terrible battery, I believe before the darkness fell on me." After a recital of Bouverie's offenses, Warfield in authorial voice rhetorically asks, "Why should a high-souled woman . . . be immured and tortured, for the sake of a reckless visionary, who had evidently forfeited his life to the laws of his country?"

The answer given was the approved one of the age: "The affection I [once] bore him could not be shaken by sin and shame—it had become one of the pillars of the temple," that is, of the sacred Victorian marriage, which only death could dissolve.[59] Throughout her tribulations, like Susan Warner's Ellen Montgomery and hundreds of other Victorian fictional heroines, Camilla remains the dutiful wife and successfully fulfills the admonition that "though we *must* sorrow, we must not rebel."[60] The duty of suffering was alleged to be the anointed role of the wife. Only occasionally did women of Catherine Warfield's generation object that their contemporaries failed to deem it as a matter of course "a strange state of things that a woman of first-rate talents, industry and integrity" should have to bear trials that a man would cringe from facing.[61]

Catherine Warfield was not entirely silent on the issue of feminine identification in an antifeminist, patriarchal culture. In the first verse of a sonnet, she once celebrated her blooming self-confidence. "Oh what joy to Stand / Enfranchised, firm, a Sovereign in the land." But by the end of the poem she reverts to doubt, wondering "Can the freed lark sing [illegible] to the stars—Whose wing was broken on its prison bars?" In another, doubt turns to dejection, but melancholy becomes itself a mark of personal uniqueness. The poet says that melancholy is so familiar a companion that it must be welcomed as a friend:

> In my despair I place my chief protection!
> Oh lead me to my prison home again.
> It suits me best to dwell amid the gloom
> of that still solitude, that living tomb
> Where sometimes in the darkness I discern
> the phantom forms I idolized so long
> And in my fetters feel my soul grow strong.[62]

In the patriarchal setting of the American South, plantation women learned early that they, too, should not display grief, sadness, or even anger in a way that reflected upon their vulnerability, their sense of honor. Nor were they, by expression of defiance against the world, to injure the pride of the men upon whom they depended. To vent one's passions was considered selfish and immoral. Hence, expressions of resentment had to be held back or spoken in a special language that deadened its personal directness. As a result, every reflection on the right of women to their own identity is countered by stern advice that women should not venture beyond the high ramparts of convention. Catherine Warfield's friend Mary Tardy pointed out the moral lesson of all the Warfield novels was that "intellect without moral goodness is nothing worth," a theme that Walker Percy would sound repeatedly in his novels a hundred years later—along with the notion of redemptive suffering for both men and women.[63] Even though Warfield lacked his sophistication and technical skills, she had explored relatively new terrain in women's fiction and helped to establish a women's literary tradition of which she was herself a pioneer rather than an inheritor.

How much personal satisfaction Catherine Warfield's achievements gave her would not be easy to ascertain. Remembering a cheerless childhood under the supervision of austere governesses and a distant father and, above all, denied a mother's love, Catherine early had learned to hide her feelings. A reporter visiting her plantation, Beechmoor, in June 1868 declared that Warfield "preserves always a certain reserve and decorum of life." According to her interviewer, she was gracious in her hospitality, proud of her lineage, "and always conscious of her *own value.*" Yet she had only a few friends and never confided in them, even though she often took upon herself the problems of others. Her withdrawal from intimacy by no means contradicted that capacity to understand their pain. Yet, as the reporter remarked, "Dreams are over with her;—the experiences of life have been very sad and very bitter." Obviously the interviewer found her elusive. "At her door the god of silence stands ever with his finger on his lip," and the intruder, no matter how persuasive, would never be "allowed to lift the veil which falls before the inner life."[64]

After the Civil War, Catherine Warfield wrote several other novels, none of which achieved the popularity or complexity of *The Household of Bouverie*. In her subsequent works, notably *Ferne Fleming, The Cardinal's Daughter, Miriam Monfort*, and *The Romance of Beauseincourt*, the main action concerned the troubled bond of a young heroine to her father or to a fatherlike figure—formidable, patriarchal, and often sexually sinister. Although conventional within the romantic genre, this paradigm, so often repeated, suggested that it served what literary critic Norman Holland has called an "identity theme," affording a unity to her novels, just as Walker Percy's repetition of similar heroes, all of them lost and stricken, reflected a parallel personal agenda. Perhaps Warfield herself recognized the close relationship of her life and her art when she wrote feelingly of an admiration for Mrs. Gaskell's life of Charlotte Brontë. "That tragic and strange biography," Warfield mused, "once in a season of deep despondency did more to reconcile me to my own condition, through my pity and admiration for another, than all the condolences that came so freely from lip and pen." For Holland, the literary process often involves what Alan Roland calls "a defensive transformation of unconscious impulses and fantasies" from the various levels of one's experiences, going back to the earliest of them all in childhood.[65]

How much might Warfield have achieved if women had been educated in a disciplined and structured fashion in which her male contemporaries were. As it was, she had been hindered not only by the constraints that female delicacy forced upon women writers but also by her lack of experience in the world of men. Even if she had been more thoroughly immersed in racetrack life alongside her sporting husband Elisha, her sense of rigid propriety would have prevented her exploitation of that arena in her fiction. She did, however, make use of tragic events that she herself had witnessed. In her novel *The Romance of Beauseincourt* (1867), for instance, Marcelline, the heroine, was reportedly drawn from life, and the death of the repulsive Colonel La Vigne in a swamp with his eyes picked out by vultures came from an incident on a plantation in Florida adjacent to Major Ware's during one of young Catherine's visits there in the late 1820s or early 1830s.[66]

With such materials—including her personal and familial experiences with the ravages of madness—she as well as Ellen Lee accomplished much. A family tradition had begun, curiously on the distaff side of this conservative, patriarchal Southern family. The "Two Sisters of the West" prepared the way for their protegé and niece Sarah Ellis Dorsey. Dorsey would write an outstanding work of history, unjustly neglected, although her five romances show a rigid adherence to formula that Warfield's *Household of Bouverie* had partially surmounted. The sisters also inspired a fourth Percy-descended fiction writer, Ellen's only daughter Sarah Catherine Ferguson, a lively if ill-starred novelist of the 1880s. Kate, as she was called, was the last of the female writers in the Percy strain, the tragicomic subject of the next chapter. Like Edna Earle Ponder in Eudora Welty's *The Ponder Heart* in Lucinda MacKethan's elegant interpretation, the last of the Percy women writers only seemed to have had a happier and more fulfilling life than her mother's or her Aunt Catherine's.[67]

Chapter Two

KATE FERGUSON, SCANDAL, AND PERCY MYTHMAKING

The story of Kate Ferguson
of Greenville, Mississippi, reveals much more
about Southern literary life than her almost total obscurity
and lack of productivity would ever suggest. She wrote only
one novel, and it is not very good. *Cliquot* lacks the polish
of her aunt Catherine Warfield's sentimental warhorses
and has a matter-of-factness missing from the trills of her
mother Ellen Lee's verses. Why should even a few pages be
devoted to so minor a player on the late Victorian literary
stage in an isolated, malarial Mississippi River port?

Three reasons emerge to rescue this novelist from the
dustbin of literary chronicles. First, the telling of her story
shows how different the writing of history is from what it
was just a few years ago, thanks to that often-maligned
ideology of feminism and an increasing awareness of how
problematic the exploration of "factual" history has become. Most historians used to be completely unselfcon-
scious about their craft. Their task was merely to collect a
suitable number of notes from which accumulation a fitting
interpretation was supposed to appear. Reinterpretations
of events or lives were based on the notion that the older
versions had lacked the proper number or arrangement of
the facts. Influenced by the self-questioning taking place
in English, historians recognize the problematic nature of
their enterprise and yet are free from the old constraints,
so that almost anything can be called a fact if it sheds light
on the new kinds of problems we ask about the past. This
account helps to illustrate the point.

The second reason for treating this almost anonymous
Southern female author seriously is that her story dem-

onstrates why a late-nineteenth-century woman with un-
doubted talent failed so catastrophically. The explanation
is twofold: Kate Ferguson was a victim of a family tragedy
and a captive of a transitional literary moment. She did
not have the advantage of her aunt and mother, who met
the low expectations to which all women writers had been
earlier assigned. As her racy style of life in the post–Civil
War New South suggested, Ferguson considered herself
liberated from the confining innocence of her literary fore-
mothers Ellen Lee, Catherine Warfield, and Sarah Dorsey,
writers previously discussed or mentioned. Yet in terms of
literary genres open to women writers, no clear guidelines
had surfaced. She did not have the education, sophistication, self-confidence, or freedom from marital responsibilities to place herself in a class with Kate Chopin, her
contemporary. From her story we gain insight into the
pleasures, anxieties, and insecurities of the era and how
those circumstances brought to a close the female writing
tradition in the Percy clan.

Finally, and no less important because it leads toward
a fresh consideration of Walker Percy in the final chapter, one can see how a family's selective amnesia wiped
out the whole story of Kate and her foremothers Ellen and
Catherine. Instead the Percy clan, especially Will Percy,
Walker's cousin and guardian, made a heroic tale out of the
disgrace of Kate's husband to rescue the family's tarnished
honor. All these things were interconnected in a poignant
and melancholy exercise.

Like her mother Eleanor Percy Lee, Kate Ferguson had
literary aspirations, and they matched the style of life she
enjoyed. In 1888 she published *Cliquot*, a romance with a

racing and indeed racy theme—as the literary standards then were. Indeed, if Sarah Dorsey, Kate's first cousin, had read it she would have labeled *Cliquot* decidedly "impure." Neil Emory, the hero, is a wealthy planter who owns a nervous but speedy stallion, Cliquot, which has killed several jockeys before Emory finds someone capable of riding the horse to easy victory. The mysterious jockey, who wins the owner a fortune that frees him from a villainous moneylender and silences a racing rival, turns out to be the beautiful heroine in disguise, Gwendoline Gwinn, Cliquot's former owner. But the hero is already spoken for. Celia, his alcoholic wife, abruptly reappears to dash his hopes for breaking the tie on grounds of desertion. After some further complications of the plot, she conveniently dies in his arms of consumption.

The story might be called one of the early examples of the bodice-ripping style. In this fiction, female bosoms tended to heave with open desire, and heroes expressed their love in ways that an earlier generation would have found much too suggestive. Even in the conservative South, women readers, to whom *Cliquot* was meant to appeal, were much more secular—and sensual—in their tastes than their mothers had been. Kate's Aunt Catherine had published most of her romances with J. B. Peterson and Brothers, a Philadelphia firm, but they had never gushed about her tame stories in the way they did about *Cliquot*. The blurb promised a story "full of passion, piquancy and breathless interest." It was, the editor went on, "chic," a word newly imported from the unvirtuous French.

By identifying the "rising young Southern authoress" as a member of "the Amélie Rives school," the publishers looked for the high sales that novelist Rives had recently achieved with her sensational (for the time) depictions of female sensuality and implied equality with the men they hungered for. Rives, about whom we know thanks to Wayne Mixon's penetrating essay, represented a surprisingly modern development in Southern female letters in the closing years of the century. She was no cheap exploiter with low origins and little education, but rather an aristocratic Virginian whose godfather at her christening in 1863 was General Robert E. Lee himself.[1] Kate Ferguson strove to imitate Rives's rebellion against conventionality in both her style of living and the character of her fiction. Rives once had a fictional character declare that women "are not the bloodless creatures we are generally thought to be," but, in repression of actuality, "we are trained to regard all healthy, natural, vivid impulses as unrefined, unfeminine, immodest." Kate Ferguson heartily agreed with such sentiments, un-Percylike, un-Southern though they were.[2]

Whereas Warfield, Lee, and Dorsey dealt with the proper fictional world of attorneys, planters, and litterateurs, Kate Ferguson chose the distinctly risqué sporting scene, but one with a degree of realism about the life that Kate herself knew intimately. In her novel, gamblers get drunk and fight, mothers connive to marry their daughters to wealthy, idle old men, and extramarital sexual relations between Neil Emory and Gwendoline Gwinn are coyly implied. Lacing her tale with anti-Victorian spice, Ferguson was intentionally rejecting the long-standing formula of having a Southern girl chastely fall in love with a gallant Union officer during the war. Noting the change that was taking place, historian Michael O'Brien has ventured to call the late-nineteenth-century crop of writers—the young Ellen Glasgow, Kate Chopin, Joel Chandler Harris, and George W. Cable—a signal for a " 'renaissance' as real to the literary critics" of that era "as the more celebrated 'Southern Literary Renaissance' of the 1930s."[3]

Ferguson does not belong in O'Brien's literary pantheon, but she felt the same sense of renewal and freedom from the old restraints that those he mentioned did. As a result, unlike her literary predecessors in the family, she did not justify her fiction with periodic moral pronouncements. Instead, Ferguson fashioned a decidedly androgynous heroine, as if to say that women were as capable of action, lust, and craftiness as men. The novel reflected the temperament of its author and shows surprising narrative talent and energy. Her fast-paced dialogues and quick studies of character suggest that she might have developed as an artist beyond the literary skill of her foremothers.

In part, Ferguson's brief success lay in her knowledge of the world she was describing. In contrast, Warfield, Lee, and Dorsey had been unable to handle the alien world of men with much authenticity. The younger novelist belonged in the racetrack setting about which she wrote. Gwendoline Gwinn, the disguised jockey, was undoubtedly drawn to resemble in spirit and interest Kate Ferguson's own daughter, Natalie. In *Lanterns on the Levee* Will Percy remembered watching Natalie astride her horse wearing "a long black velvet riding habit" that made her the handsomest horsewoman in the district.[4] Ironically, Ferguson was introduced to the racing scene by the Warfields of Kentucky. Catherine Warfield had been her guardian after Ellen's death from yellow fever in 1849. Elisha Warfield, Catherine's husband, bred racehorses, and his father had been a founder of the Lexington, Kentucky, racetrack. Yet Catherine herself had never dared to write about jockeys, bookmakers, and "gentlemen of leisure" who smoked cigars, wenched, and drank toddies. The source of reality that gave Kate a sense of literary verisimilitude would also be the origin of her downfall.

Despite her rebellion against old-fashioned prudery, Kate Ferguson was appropriately proud of her literary fore-mothers. Doubtless she considered *Cliquot* a first start in her contribution to a female tradition in the family. She had already honored the memory of her mother by having Ellen's poem "The Eagle" used as a means to venerate her first cousin Confederate Colonel William Alexander Percy, whom grandson Will Percy calls "Fafar" in *Lanterns on the Levee.* During the war the colonel was dubbed "the Gray Eagle of the Delta" for his daring assaults. Moreover, Kate believed that she was perpetuating another Percy tradition, that of martial valor, by marrying a war hero. Samuel Wragg Ferguson had led a local cavalry troop that harassed the enemy around Greenville. A glorious symbol of the "Lost Cause," he had been raised to general "at an age," Will Percy noted, "when others were lucky to be captains." General Ferguson was later to be his wife's nemesis, but at the time *Cliquot* appeared, Samuel and the lively Kate were the center of a political and social set in Greenville, the activities of which deserve attention because it was the source of her literary, social, and financial downfall and also because it signaled the end of the female literary tradition in the family.

The early postwar years had been trying times in the Delta as elsewhere in the Confederate South. Plantations lay in ruins and, to the chagrin of former slaveowners, the work force had become free and unsubmissive. After the Mississippi Redeemer Democrats forced the so-called black Republicans from office in 1876, however, attorney William Alexander Percy and his cousin-in-law Ferguson formed a powerful clique of large-scale planters that ran Washington County politics. Under Colonel Percy's leadership, the Levee Board was significant not only because of its work in flood control but also because, through contracts for construction, it provided a foundation for patronage and power—from day laborers and foremen to various professional groups of engineers, lawyers, and accountants. As a friend of the Redeemer governors, Colonel Percy, and then LeRoy, his law partner and son, uniformly had control of appointments, so that Ferguson's assignment as treasurer of the Delta Levee Board had been easy to arrange.[5]

After the Gray Eagle died in 1888 at an early age, LeRoy stepped fully into his political shoes, ran the board and other local institutions to the benefit of the faction and the satisfaction of Percy's corporate clients in the state, most especially the railroads that connected the Delta to Chicago and New Orleans. Yet these were anxious times. Prices for cotton fluctuated wildly, racial strife was growing ever more violent, and scandals of bribery and embezzlement rocked Southern state governments.[6] As if to banish such disagreeable realities, the local elite developed a giddy style of life. Greenville was very much a river town, with a much more heterogeneous population than could be found elsewhere in the state. Among the scattering of Chinese, Italian, German, and Irish immigrants, there was the anomalous family of Comptons: Eliza and her granddaughters. Eliza was the light-skinned daughter of a Louisiana planter and his quadroon mistress. After seeing to her education in New Orleans, the plantation magnate allowed his white overseer to marry her and gave them a small farm near Greenville that Eliza called "Egypt" in celebration of her freedom. Her daughter Ann lived with overseer Compton's nephew in a tangle of miscegenated intimacies. Eliza, however, took an inheritance from the old Louisiana planter and bought herself a spacious house in Greenville. She brought her three attractive grand-daughters up from the farm to be her companions and the receptacle of her own family ambitions. Thus, her purpose was twofold: to earn a good living as a caterer for the rich and to marry off nearly white Emma, Laura, and Sarah to the wealthy bachelors who amused themselves at the house.[7] The set to which Kate Ferguson and her pleasure-seeking husband belonged made the Compton house in Greenville their sometime social headquarters.

The Comptons' ties to the Fergusons and Percys help to make the future undoing of the General and his wife Kate more understandable. We know what went on at the Comptons' because Harry Ball, a penniless young bache-lor, kept a lengthy and detailed diary. He belonged on the fringes of the Percy clique and recorded its affairs almost daily.[8] Grandmother Eliza trained the young Comp-ton women, recounted Ball, "in all the arts of fascination" which Eliza herself had learned at a finishing school pro-vided by her Louisiana father, so that the girls acquired "the air and manner of ladies of pleasure." Each of them had a different kind of charm and beauty. Emma was slender and sprightly, Laura tall, handsome and dignified; Sarah, known as Ching, had the whitest skin. "Old Eliza took the most egregious pride in them," Ball recorded. "She was well to do, and did not hesitate to levy con-tributions from her visitors."[9] General Ferguson and his wife were living well beyond their funds, a good portion of which entered the Comptons' cash box in payment of catering services and other amenities.

None but the most important people in society went to "Aunt Liza's," where they could count on Creole cuisine, good wines, and the hostess's discretion about what went on in the upstairs bedrooms. "Among the most constant visitors," Ball recalled, "were . . . LeRoy Percy . . . General Ferguson and Downs Pace, at that time the swellest beau in Greenville," after the death of his wife Fannie Percy, LeRoy's sister. Harry Ball remembered that upon arrival at ten one evening Laura Compton greeted him quickly and, without saying another word, beckoned him into the dining room. There he was surprised to see Kate Ferguson at the all-male-guest establishment. Her presence without her husband was a serious breach of the Victorian code. She was seated at the very head of the dining-room table, which was loaded with food, punch, wines, lights, and flowers. Aside from the servants and the Comptons, Kate was the only woman present. "She was," said Ball, "a perfect Mrs Reiner or Mrs Hanksbee, or Lena Despard—a natural born adventuress and mantra, but her social position was such that nothing she did could injure it much." Kate knew that the gentlemen at Aunt Liza's would never gossip to their wives. "General Ferguson himself came later, and they greeted each other with easy camaraderie," Ball remembered. "It is hard to say which of them was the worst, but they were charming people, all the same. She spoiled the supper. The girls were timid and the fun was forced until 1 a m when Mrs F. was taken home in a carriage by [Downs] Pace, both very drunk, and the general making no demur." [10]

In 1886 Kate astonished Ball once again—at an amateur production of "Sea of Ice," a popular drama of the day. Among those on stage were young "Willie" Percy, LeRoy's brother, Duegue Ferguson, Kate and the General's son, and Kate herself. The performance was supposed to be high melodrama, but turned into unintended farce. The audience laughed at the most "affecting" points. The cause of much hilarity was Kate Ferguson, who was, "at her ripe age, assuming the part of a young Indian maid, in very inadequate clothing—her kirtle only coming down to the knees on one side, and not that far on the other, with bare arms, bare bosom, bare legs, and big bracelets round her ankles." [11]

Unlike her prim and serious-minded Aunt Catherine, Kate Ferguson liked to be the center of male attention. When Harry Ball went to a New Year's Day reception at Robertshaw, the Fergusons' elegant house adjacent to the Percys', he found "a conglomeration of rowdy, half-drunken men, and herself the only woman. Punch flowed, and madame danced with all the men, one after another, except me, who pleaded my foundered feet & tight shoes." After witnessing only a few minutes of the scene, Camille Percy, the dignified and exquisite wife of LeRoy Percy, was so horrified that she bade her husband and Harry Ball to take her home next door. [12]

Under these circumstances, an almost Biblical retribution awaited the hapless Fergusons. Although treasurer of the Delta Levee Board, the General had no knowledge of accounting and even less business aptitude, to which deficiencies he added healthy portions of caprice and inattentiveness. [13] On July 9, 1894, the Levee Board discussed a mistake that the finance committee members had found in the books. Ferguson admitted error but promised, if re-elected, to make no more. But the decision was reached to have an investigation of all the books by a competent accountant. Board member W. A. Everman, himself an accountant, discovered to his indignation a discrepancy of $39,000 or more in the ledgers.[14] "Like a disjointed pin-wheel," recalled Will Percy, Everman, though a member of the Percy inner circle, raced about the town spreading the word of the General's dishonesty.[15]

LeRoy and the others in the faction were highly embarrassed. As a leading member of the Percy circle, Captain J. S. McNeily, editor of the Greenville *Times* and another kinsman of the Percys, tried to excuse his colleague. In the paper he argued that the Levee Board members had been overly "absorbed in and depressed over their own affairs" during the current economic depression and had become "to a degree unmindful of their public duty." The problems were, he continued, a slipshod method of oversight and a tendency to place faith in personal expressions of honor, while neglecting "prescribed checks and rules." He could not, however, explain where the money had gone.[16] Only a week earlier General Ferguson had stood high on the list of those credited with "untarnished honor," a theme that might be called the Confederate hero's very specialty. Ferguson held the post of Chancellor Commander of the Knights of Pythias, was dubbed a Knight Templar in the Masonic Order, and joined both the Legion of Honor and the Knights of Honor.[17]

These memberships did not save him from the humiliation of a public meeting which he shrank from attending. In his absence LeRoy Percy and other conservative associates did their best to keep an indignant crowd in check.[18]

When LeRoy relinquished the floor, Judge Wynn, another member of the clique, announced that Duegue Ferguson, the General's son, and Kate, his wife, were both willing to sacrifice all their property—houses and lands—to make up the loss to the taxpayers. The crowd was appeased, but Judge Wynn could not forbear an appeal to their sense of chivalry: " 'Do you, fellow men, want to see an old man, bowed with age, in delicate health—those of you especially who wore the gray in the times of distress, see the man who led you in the thick of battle, he whom you honored and loved—wear the stripes of a felon, and be imprisoned in a felon's cell?' " Then, hoping to save the humiliated Kate, he implored, " 'Do you want to see this good woman who signed these notes, who has given up the old homestead, the roof over her head, and who has not saved a meal of victuals which she can call her own, to pay the delinquencies of her husband, to suffer more distress than which she is now passing through? I say it was a noble action on the part of the Board to accept it, and the whole matter should rest there.' Loud and continuous applause." [19]

Kate Lee Ferguson must have found some consolation in Judge Wynn's depiction of the family's response. But compounding her sense of shame was her husband's abrupt disappearance, even as the voices of his friends were pouring balm into the wounds of Ferguson family pride. The veteran officer, who had once gallantly harassed Sherman's troops as they progressed toward Savannah, could not face his fellow citizens directly. Instead, he slipped out of town, not to surface again until he reached Tambillo in the mountains of Ecuador.[20] Kate Ferguson, a virtual widow, continued to live in Greenville, but she never wrote another line of literary prose. Her confidence had fled with her absconding husband's honor to a remote village in the Andes. She died in 1907, a figure of local pity.

The third element in this deconstructed account of reality, gender, and myth was the interpretation with which the Percy clan endowed so sad a story of familial disgrace. The account has a distinctly masculine texture. According to Will Percy, a curious incident occurred not long after Kate Ferguson's death. Home from Harvard Law School for the holidays, Will and some of his classmates and a group of local belles were gathered at the dinner table with his parents. All the young people, Will reminisced, were attired in their "giddiest" for a dance afterwards. They heard a knock at the door. Out of the cold night air there appeared in the room a small, shabbily dressed figure sporting a flashy necktie. His beard was unkempt and his white hair dirty. The stranger had a vacant but glowing look in his eyes. When LeRoy Percy saw him enter the room, he exclaimed softly, "Why, General Ferguson! Come in." Heartily urged to join the guests for dinner, Will continued, he pulled up a chair and cast a pall on the entertainment as if he were "Banquo's ghost." Soon the young guests returned to their silliness, but Will noticed that his mother was about to weep. Ferguson leaned over and whispered to LeRoy that he had returned to reexamine "those old records. It was all a mistake," he croaked hollowly. "They will show everything was in order." With typical Southern courtesy, LeRoy Percy replied without a moment's hesitation, "Of course, General." For the next week or so Ferguson scuttled about the courthouse and the office of the Levee Board, studi-

---

ously jotting down notes from dust-covered ledgers. Then once again he drifted off, to be seen no more.[21]

Rendering this account in his classic memoir *Lanterns on the Levee,* Will Percy, LeRoy's ever-loyal son, endowed the episode with all the pathos and humor that he could manage. He wished to show how friendship, loyalty, and good breeding combined in those better times to create a world of masculine camaraderie, stability, and decency. Will found it highly admirable that during the height of the scandal a diminutive friend of the Percy family named Merritt Williams had defended the General's honor, stained though it was. As Percy told the story, Williams overheard two passengers on a steamboat denouncing the General. As they dined, the pair refused to heed Williams's request for them to stop insulting his friend. Exasperated, the slight-framed gentleman struck one of the strangers directly between the eyes with a heavy coffee pot and with blows to the jaw decked the partner next to the first. Asked about it years later, "Mr. Merritt," he wrote, "said it was just a little personal matter." [22] That, in the opinion of the Delta elite, Will Percy concluded, was the way to handle such an unpleasantness.

Percy's account of the Ferguson incident was, alas, largely fanciful, but the rationale for such seemingly self-serving narratives as his must be understood. Claude Levi-Strauss, the great French anthropologist, argues that "the purpose of myth is to provide a local model capable of overcoming a contradiction." [23] In telling General Ferguson's story Will Percy sought to show that even at their worst his forefathers lived by ethical standards that a more secular, desacralized world of machines and nameless masses could never recapture. His championing of the old defaulter and his father's other friends was meant to be a reminder that friendship and loyalty had their place in the moral order. Honor once mattered, Will Percy affirmed.

The contemporary critics who reviewed *Lanterns on the Levee* in 1941 failed to notice its imaginative elements and assumed that Percy's object was to tell a factually accurate but sympathetic account of the glorious Southern past with its rich code of manners and chivalry. Yet in telling the story of Ferguson's plunge into ruin, mysterious reappearance like a spirit from the netherworld, and his parents' poignant reactions to the old man's protestations of innocence, Will Percy sought to stress the connection between insanity and personal honor in men. He wished to compare that connection with the amorality and normality of modern life. "People steal public funds now, but the public is cynical, no one is horrified, and the accused, guilty or innocent, seldom goes mad" as Ferguson did, the memorialist preached. "Going mad for honor's sake presupposes honor. In our brave new world a man of honor is rather like the Negro—there's no place for him to go." [24]

What the author implies by his racial observation is that to violate the ethic of an honor-bound social order is so irreparable, so stigmatizing that it leads to derangement, a wholly fitting punishment. A branding of the mind, as it were, attests to the transgressor's guilt forever, but somehow dignity, however shabbily attired, remains. Will Percy is also implying that a society which ignores honor is more benighted than one that drives its outcasts to lunacy.

One suspects that Percy himself identified with the mad sinner of his literary creation, not because the memorialist had ever violated a public trust in the fashion of General Ferguson, but because, though the heroic LeRoy Percy's son, he always felt to be an outsider. He was an intellectual and a poet, preoccupations that others in that hard-minded planter society considered unmanly—the playthings of women like Kate Ferguson but far from the important world of politics, money, and gentlemanly sport. His father LeRoy certainly thought so, and made his contempt for his son's aestheticism a source of constant tension between the pair.

As if to compensate for this sometimes voiced disapproval, Will Percy made himself the champion of his father and his friends, good and bad. Having first portrayed Ferguson as an ex-Confederate Cervantean figure with scruffy beard and distracted behavior, the author momentarily escapes from his half-satirical account by issuing a didactic sermon on the indifference to vice and the immorality of the current age. He contrasts the present-day "mental cripples, the moral anemics" with his father's friends "Cap Mac [Captain McNeily] and General Catchings." Such paladins as these, he recklessly asserts, somehow managed to be "at once Puritans and Cavaliers." Even more excessively, he declared that they "would have been at home on the west portal of Chartres with those strong ancients, severe and formidable and full of grace, who guard the holy entrance."[25] The transition to extravagance was too incongruous to be convincing. The notion of General Thomas L. Catchings, a retired Delta congressman with the political charm of cold soup, and McNeily, the small-town editor, as figures monumental enough to embellish a French cathedral careened toward the ludicrous. The reader is not meant to laugh. Yet Percy's characterization inadvertently parodied the sometimes pretentious romanticism of the white South.

Intentional or not, the trope made room for irony and ambivalence. On the one hand, Will Percy's analogy reaffirmed his reverence for his father, who, living or dead, remained, in the son's view, a stern monitor of his son's character. The memorialist did so by situating LeRoy Percy's circle of friends in the midst of the grim-faced and virile warriors of stone. In the next paragraph, however, Percy half recognized the absurdity himself. Quickly he slipped into a different guise, taking off the hair shirt of the antimodernist Jeremiah. In its place he donned the short pants of the precocious, well-read boy listening to his elders—as if they, he says, were "the patriarchs of Chartres sipping the dregs of a julep." Meantime his mother Camille presides over this madcap cocktail hour as "the Queen of Sheba," another figure from the cathedral statuary.[26] Thus in a few lines of text Percy moved from humor to pathos, from moral indignation to outrageous hyperbole, and from there to mock-heroic absurdity. This kind of narrative complexity can be detected throughout the work. *Lanterns on the Levee* is a series carefully constructed, inconsistent layers of hidden emotions, idealistic fancies, and sad reflections.

Did Percy intend such complications, ones that he hid even from himself? Unlike William Faulkner, Vladimir Nabokov, or other practitioners of what might be called heroic satire, Percy was probably unaware of these ambiguities and subversive undertones. His correspondence with his friend Gerstle Mack, the New York art historian, was most revealing. He sent him a draft of the book while it was still incomplete in 1939. In response Mack lambasted his racial views and criticized him, as Will phrased it, for being "a professional Southerner and the manuscript as a

kind of defense of the South." At once, Percy invoked a dis-
claimer, particularly regarding the Levee Board treasurer
whose depiction Mack thought betrayed a regional senti-
mentality and obfuscation of moral values. Percy replied,
"You do not like the General Ferguson episode and think
it destroys my thesis." Of course, he rejoined, Ferguson's
defalcation did not speak well of "the aristocratic cast that
I had been praising." Yet he was trying, he told Mack, to
convey "the tragedy" of the affair that he knew his parents
believed it to be.

Will Percy was too young at the time to realize how Kate
and Samuel Ferguson had been overspending themselves,
like addicted gamblers who seek subconsciously their own
ruin. Then, probably to Mack's perplexity, Percy declared
that, of course, Southern aristocrats "were full of flaws,"
but, he also professed, they "need no defense." With one
hand he gave away his case, with the other he took it
back again. Percy meant that under the code of honor,
their assumption of moral superiority, not their deeds, de-
fined, elevated, and defended them. They were exactly
what they claimed to be so that even in their weakness they
were still morally supreme over the blind and thoughtless
mass of mankind. No attorney was required to prove what
was manifest to him. Will's closing line to his Manhattan
friend was meant to put the matter to rest: "So you see,
though melancholy, I am not silenced." [27] The fundamental
inconsistencies escaped him.

What is most conspicuous about the story is the absence
of any reference to Kate Ferguson, the wife of the General whom Percy sought to ennoble. Will Percy was only
following his father's indifference to her life and fate. Kate
might have written a novel and considered herself a child

of literary mothers, but what women did in a creative way meant nothing at all to the male Percys. A writer himself—an occupation that Southerners generally thought effeminate—Will Percy did not point with pride to his cousin's achievements, but instead made a hero out of a defaulting Levee Board officer who had so lost his nerve that he could not face his fellow townspeople but left his wife and son behind to meet that obligation. Such was the selective character of honor in the South of that era. Like the dogs that failed to bark in the Sherlock Holmes mystery, we find the real meaning of the story not only in Percy's elaborations about the men—his father and General Ferguson—but also in his omission of the women writers. A similar theme of feminine neglect dominates the next chapter, but in the latter instance the feminine mode could not entirely be repressed, but found expression in Walker Percy's fiction in unexpected guises.

Chapter Three

"DESPERATE
STORYTELLING"

For Walker Percy,
as it had been for his literary predecessors
in the family, writing fiction would prove briefly liberating
from the scourge of melancholy by transferring personal
pain into imagined situations. Like Dante's wayfarer in
The Divine Comedy, he had secured the authority to write
about death and despair, having faced them directly. Virginia Woolf once explained that most authors failed to
treat such matters with much authenticity because "to look
these things squarely in the face would need the courage
of a lion-tamer; a robust philosophy; a reason rooted in
the bowels of the earth. Short of these, this monster, the
body, this miracle, its pain, will soon make us taper into
mysticism, or rise, with rapid beats of the wings, into the
raptures of transcendentalism."[1]

Percy had the fortitude that Woolf considered necessary
in a great writer. At times he tapered into mysticism, much
to the consternation of his friend and fellow novelist Shelby
Foote. "I'm lost in a welter of vague spinnings," Foote confessed to Walker after reading one of his scholarly essays
in 1956.[2] Nonetheless, a sense of irony and a basic hard-
headedness saved Percy the novelist from Woolf's deni-
grated "raptures of transcendentalism." The process of
his maturing began in his young adulthood when, in the
late 1930s, he recognized a need for professional help. A
Southerner with strong conservative leanings, he took the
unusual step of undergoing prolonged and intensive analysis with Janet Rioch, a prominent New York practitioner
who had studied with Harry Stack Sullivan, a friend of
Walker's guardian, Will Percy. The novelist claimed that he

never did work out what was precisely wrong with him in these sessions.[3] Yet he clearly appreciated the close connection between depression and his later life of imaginative writing and philosophical thought.

Toward the end of his life, in 1987, Percy told Robert Cubbage, "Carl Jung was right in encouraging his patients to believe that their anxiety and depression might be trying to tell them something of value." The signs of pain are not mere "symptoms," he continued. "It helps enormously when a person can make a friend with her terror, plumb the depths of her depression. 'There's gold down there in the darkness,' said Dr. Jung."[4] The reaction to depression stimulates a craving to write, paint, compose, or undertake some other mission of originality, an activity that can give order and meaning to an empty or shattered life. The inexpressible can be articulated through imagined forms, different voices, interlocking themes. The author is usually certain that the act of composition has primarily outward purposes—the entertainment of a readership and the sending of a message to the world. "Writing is a humble vocation," Percy told an interviewer, "he's [the writer] making up a story to divert the reader . . . but even a novelist has a right to issue a warning."[5]

Walker Percy took seriously the writer's function as moral arbiter, a role that made more difficult his discovery of a special voice that would not bore or bludgeon the reader with heavy preachment. His long apprenticeship as a writer—from 1945 or so, when he abandoned medical practice, to the late 1950s—suggests that, despite his deep analysis, finding himself in a professional way was no easy task. In fact, his years of learning the craft were much longer than that of such comparable writers as Faulkner, Hemingway, Tate, and Warren. In 1966 he offered a glimpse into how he interpreted his own development, a curious alternation between dejection and desire. The writer, he confessed, "hits on something," but after initial, hard labor fails, "there follows a period of discouragement. Then there comes a paradoxical moment of collapse-and-renewal in which one somehow breaks with the past and starts afresh." Prior drafts wind up on the floor and the counsel of friends is forgotten. "It is almost as if the discouragement were necessary, that one has first to encounter despair before one is entitled to hope."[6]

Despite these revealing comments, Percy was very close-lipped about his inner life, confiding only in Shelby Foote, his fellow novelist and friend since childhood in Greenville. Even as a youngster, declared Foote, "In repose, his face took on a certain sadness."[7] With regard to his motives for writing, Percy did not admit to any personal designs. When asked to comment if he agreed with William Faulkner that the writer "is a creature driven by demons," he replied, "I don't know. I write because it's what I want to do."[8] Nonetheless, the writer is engaged in a colloquy with his or her own work. The latter is an artifact which offers an explanation, rationale, or a gratifying outcome for some puzzling, even horrifying internal question that remains hidden beneath the texture of the work itself. With reference to Walker Percy, Jay Tolson, his biographer, put the matter brilliantly: "Percy's real work in fiction began when he gave free rein to those daemonic voices raging within him, when he allowed his lack of a central or integrated self to become his real subject."[9]

As Tolson's comment implies, the creative act does not invariably supply the artist with a new self-confidence. It does not mend the broken fabric of the interior life. As the analyst Albert Rothenberg argues, "A work of art may reduce anxiety to some extent for both creator and recipient, but it also stimulates the anxieties of both to a degree." Even though creation can serve as a means to cope with unmanageable feelings, it is "not a form of therapy." [10] It can, however, furnish a sense of power and fulfill ambition. "Profound melancholy," observes the psychiatrist Kay Redfield Jamison, "can fundamentally change an individual's expectations and beliefs about the nature, duration, and meaning of life, the nature of man, and the fragility and resilience of the human spirit." Early in his career Percy confided to his friend Shelby Foote that he felt frustrated because the neighbors thought he was a time-waster or half-crazy pedant whose writing nobody could understand. All he wanted, he continued, was to reach an audience and be recognized. Writers like Flaubert who claimed to create simply for the sake of art itself were fooling themselves. [11] In his reticence he resembled in temperament his female predecessor Catherine Warfield.

Three aspects of his development as an artist should be explored, ones which also had been significant in the literary careers of his female predecessors. The first of these concerns the broader issue of creativity and melancholy, a point that will be only briefly sketched along with some essential biographical background about his upbringing and career. The second concerns Percy's search for a father and for male guidance as a literary subject and quite probably a personal quest. That longing for an approving and godlike father is not a rare focus in Southern novels written by men—there is Thomas Wolfe's *Look Homeward, Angel,* for example, Allen Tate's *The Fathers*, William Faulkner's *The Sound and Fury*. In Percy's own family, an author's pursuit of an elusive parent was also a major theme. His filial venture paralleled the way in which Catherine Warfield and Ellen Lee had sought reconciliation with their mother through the projections of their fiction and poetry. The parental theme led him to adopt the mock-heroic genre, albeit in a modern context. The third element was the subtle and perhaps unconscious mode of handling the absent mother and dealing with the heroines in whom his hero had to show some interest.

Concerning the first matter, the relation of art and depression, much more is known today than ever before. Scientific evidence mounts that popular myths or poetic conceits about such a connection have a validity which is hard to challenge. "Great wits are sure to madness near allied; / and thin partitions do their bounds divide," wrote John Dryden, versifying the notion in the seventeenth century. "Study after study," reported the New York *Times* on October 12, 1993, "has shown that people in the arts suffer disproportionately high rates of mood disorders, particularly manic depression and major depression."[12]

Not all artists are mad or even close to it, most especially not Walker Percy. Yet he knew the state of a disordered mind intimately. His closest family connections belonged in that category of depressives of whom 20 percent kill themselves.[13] His father, LeRoy Pratt Percy, a Birmingham, Alabama, lawyer, ended his own life in July 1929. The fatality occurred twelve years after attorney Walker Percy, Sr., Roy's father and Walker's grandfather, fired a shotgun shell into his chest with a gun similar to that which his son later used. In addition, when Walker was sixteen his mother, Martha Susan Phinizy Percy, plunged her car over a bridge near Greenville, Mississippi, and drowned.[14]

Furthermore, his bachelor guardian William Alexander Percy, author of *Lanterns on the Levee*, was "one with those," declared his friend David Cohn, "who have been 'half in love with easeful Death, call'd him soft names in many a musèd rhyme.' "[15] "Uncle Will," as Walker called him, suffered from hypertension and poor health, and was to die at the relatively young age of fifty-seven in 1942 when Walker was still a young adult. As expressed in his memoir and in his many conversations with Walker Percy, Will's Stoic philosophy was a bleak doctrine of self-sacrifice without reward and barren solitude, a perspective which his adopted son found both attractive and dismaying.

Finally, Walker Percy himself contracted tuberculosis while a resident at Bellevue Hospital in New York. The illness had a seriously depressing effect. It delayed and finally ended his medical career and also precluded him from entering military service in the 1940s. That hardship, as it must be called, deprived him the chance to fulfill a strong familial heritage: martial valor, including the war experiences of Walker's own father Roy. In his work, consumption was to symbolize, writes biographer Jay Tolson, "something worse than physical death: death-in-life, or despair."[16]

The adoption of a fitting literary genre for dealing with these issues would preoccupy the future novelist from 1945 to the late 1950s. Walker Percy adopted the mock-heroic because in its modern incarnation the genre is chiefly devoted to a son's coming to terms with an alienating or absent father. Literary critic Roger Salomon calls the form "desperate storytelling." [17] The phrase suggests an irresistible compulsion to explain to himself and to others those personal issues too stark for direct confrontation. Walker Percy belongs in the category with other depressive practitioners: Cervantes, Lawrence Sterne, Lord Byron, Stendhal (Marie-Henri Beyle), James Joyce, Vladimir Nabokov, Saul Bellow, and Percy's own find, John Kennedy Toole, author of *A Confederacy of Dunces.* The mock-heroic concerns a young male character who seeks to overcome obstacles in his filial past to find his identity, learn to live by the code of honor, and find a suitable mate, issues that Percy himself faced in his own development.

The genre must be broadly conceived and not identified simply with writers of the Renaissance and eighteenth century. Seeing connections between the modern forms and their predecessors, Salomon argues that the mock-heroic involves an ironic, skeptical view of two powerful, intertwined myths in Western society. They are ones that Southern whites had long held dear: the political and martial legend of the Great Hero, a transforming figure like those of Arthur's knights of old; Thomas More, Percy's favorite saint; the Cavaliers of the English Civil War, from whom Southerners liked to claim descent; and of course Robert E. Lee. But that kind of heroism is no longer possible in a secular and industrial society, so that efforts to achieve old-fashioned glory, often of a military but always aggressively masculine character, are doomed to fail.

Perhaps the martial form of escape from complexity, doubt, and ambiguity was what Will Percy had meant when he reflected in his memoir *Lanterns on the Levee* that war took on a meaning that his ordinary existence could not supply. For Walker's guardian, warfare was an enterprise in which the participants shared its ideals, miseries, and infrequent small triumphs, whereas prosaic living was "isolated and lonely." [18] As Willa Cather writes in her novel of the First World War, *One of Our Own*, many of those with "beautiful beliefs" died in battle years before they might have been overtaken with disillusion. Unluckier were those veterans, formerly officers, "whose names made the blood of youth beat faster," she writes. "One by one they quietly die by their own hand." Walker's father, like Will Percy a veteran of the First World War, was one of those *not* saved from desolating disappointment. Roy Percy had been a flying instructor. He always regretted that the war ended before he could be sent overseas. [19] In *The Moviegoer*, published in 1961, Binx Bolling does not lose his father to suicide, but rather to war, as if he were one of those of whom Cather had written. John Bolling's death as an airman over Crete in 1940 leaves Binx to be reared by his greataunt Emily Cutrer when he was fourteen, a replication of Walker's own experience. [20]

As in most modern mock-heroics, self-discovery in Percy's fiction often begins with the pursuit of intimacy with a father, but the *right* father is never really found. Aunt Emily rears Binx for some fifteen years as his father rather than mother and is even referred to as "a female sport of a fierce warrior gens," who, after her rather soldierly career with the Red Cross in the Spanish civil war, married and became "as handsome and formidable as her brothers." [21] But the author regards Aunt Emily as a most unsuitable role model. Although attached to her, Binx reacts to her constant blandishments with the passive resistance of a child; he tunes her out. [22]

Almost as if addressing Uncle Will, the novelist provides

a telling exchange. Aunt Emily appeals to memories of evenings shared years before: "Don't you remember discovering Euripides and Jean-Christophe?" But the nephew replies, " 'You discovered them for me." He feels overcome with a paralyzing lethargy. "It requires an effort to put one foot in front of the other." The symptoms suggest the depth of unspoken loss, incompleteness, and even youth's boredom with the talk of older people. The reader is not given much explanation for Binx's malaise except as a general social phenomenon, the "everydayness," as Percy called it, of ordinary living. Binx smells acutely the stench of modern life, but his inner deadness is far greater than that of the dull world he sees around him.[23] His sense of ennui is a traditional feature of the mock-heroic in which the hero finds the social order—be it aristocratic or bourgeois—stultifying, shallow, meaningless. His routines of life are insufficiently stimulating. Yet in Binx Bolling, we may infer, an additional source of alienation was the absence of a genuine and assisting father, for whom the son grieves without fully knowing it.[24]

The second aspect of the mock-heroic involves an almost religious faith in romanticism, "with its promise of the godlike possibilities open to passionate and imaginative selfhood," as Salomon argues. In mock-heroic works, the concept of the hero and the principle of romanticism are both subjected to satiric challenge. In literary terms, humor and alienation are closely allied. The mock hero does not reject society outright but rather senses an isolating discrepancy between contemporary conventions and the striving for personal uniqueness, a cleavage that reduces the hero to moments of emptiness and despair.[25]

Nearly all of Percy's fiction belongs in this ambivalently

tragicomic convention by which means Percy deals with one or another aspect of familial history as a way for him to express rage, puzzlement, and grief over his parental deprivations. In other words, art and depression were closely interlocked, and through that process he was enabled to contribute so much to American literature. Percy's response to personal anguish sets his work apart from most other leading figures in the national canon. He translated suicidal and despairing thought into depictions of how people may reach out in spiritual hunger but present their dilemmas in a comic way. As it emerges in artistic form, his own self-doubt captures the imagination of modern readers, particularly those beset with similar feelings.[26]

Walker Percy's use of the mock-heroic involves the question of a youth's sense of himself as a man, a concern that is manifest in his relation to his father and his father's values. As critics have long observed, Aunt Emily was inspired by Walker's guardian Will Percy, and, like Will himself, she utters in almost comic fashion the outmoded language of Stoic duty that Binx struggles to escape in his pursuit of his own destiny.[27] "No, my young friend, I am not ashamed to use the word class," preaches Aunt Emily. "More than anything else I wanted to pass on to you the one heritage of the men of our family." Summing up Will Percy's code derived from the meditations of the Emperor Marcus Aurelius, Walker Percy has Emily characterize that tradition as "a certain quality of spirit, a gaiety, a sense of duty, a nobility to be worn lightly, a sweetness, a gentleness with women—the only good things the South ever had and the only things that matter in this life."[28]

In *The Last Gentleman*, which followed *The Moviegoer*,

Percy made more explicit his recognition of the mock hero's paternal dilemma. He turned from a satirical perspective on his Uncle Will to a darker and more primal encounter with his father Roy in fictional form. For much of the novel the "young engineer," Will Barrett, represses his feelings about his parent and instead confusedly seeks to live up to the masculine prescriptions of Southern honor upon which his family has reared him. In the tradition of the mock-heroic, the hero constantly misreads the social conventions and makes a fool of himself in the name of honor. Barrett vainly tries to "have a face to face showdown in the street like his grandfather" with a snobbish Princeton under-graduate, but his adversary simply ignores him. Barrett blows up a memorial to the Union dead on the campus, but no one even notices. He visits old Civil War battle sites in the Shenandoah Valley. In his emotional confusion, however, he forgets who he is and has to be rescued from his fugue states that demonstrate just how repressed his traumatic memories have become.[29]

The young hero pays a heavy price for his reluctance to meet the paternal adversary: he cannot continue his psychoanalytic therapy in New York, and immaturely mocks Dr. Gamov's amusing imperfections; he passively drifts into the life of the Chandler Vaught family, seek-ing particularly in the suicidal Sutter Vaught a surrogate father to advise and comfort him; he suffers from mental and physical signs of deep depression—spasms of amne-sia, fainting spells, tics and knee-twitchings, but above all, an inability to let down his guard and enjoy with an equal partner the intimacies of love in its physical and emotional meanings. And yet, like other mock heroes, he has an uncanny facility for locating people he meets in the right class or place of origin, a sensitivity that Walker Percy exploits with telling effect.

Equally disastrous, Will Barrett, like other Percy heroes, cannot relinquish a deeply introverted self-consciousness. The mock hero in *The Last Gentleman* and his successors observe themselves as they act because they are imagining how others are perceiving them. Spontaneity of feeling and action become problematic. In a confrontation with some racists at Levittown, "strive as he might to keep his anger pure and honorable, it was no use." Suspicious of his motives, an irate resident of the town hits him hard on the nose, already swollen from an undignified attack of hay fever.[30] Only occasionally does Will Barrett in *The Last Gentleman* actually win a small victory for the old code of his ancestors. Back in Ithaca, Mississippi, where he feels more at home, he beats up a town deputy to aid some comic friends escape. For once, crisis frees him for action. "Upside down as always, he could think only when thinking was impossible. It was when thinking was expected of one that he couldn't think."[31]

Behind these feints and evasions that constantly trip the hero into ludicrous or misapprehended situations, Will Barrett is finally able to recall the last meeting with his father. He recollects how Ed Barrett had stood up to the mob, but the father is too despairing to celebrate with his followers. Repeating the strain of noble defeat that runs through Will Percy's *Lanterns on the Levee*, Walker has Ed Barrett tell his son that the enemy forces had gone, not because good had won over evil but because "they found out that we are like them." At an earlier time, the father continues, they were the cheats and thieves and "we were not," and so they despised the better class, but now everyone was corrupt and so "they know they don't have to kill me." Young Barrett feels the chill of a night that was supposed to be filled with the happy noises of victory. Instead: "(Victory is the saddest of all, said the father)"—another variant on one of Will Percy's favorite themes.[32] The father goes up to the attic and there shoots himself, leaving his son feeling betrayed and angry.

Although Percy does not have the son become aware of it, clearly Ed Barrett, consciously or not, wishes to undermine the self-confidence of his son by making it seem that nothing matters, not a hopeful message for a young man as he begins the long trek through life. Of what use are the virtues of bravery and male camaraderie in such circumstances? At one time Percy identified Binx Bolling as a "Quentin Compson who didn't commit suicide," but actually the analogy works better with Will Barrett and his father rather than Binx and his Aunt Emily, who is not suicidal and not cynical about present and future. Faulkner's character in *The Sound and Fury* has been reduced to impotence and in-turning fury by a father who had lost all feeling for life or human relations.[33] Like Ed Barrett, Jason Compson tells his son Quentin not to look for solutions. "One has no force, no authority to act in this matter because one has no originality."[34]

In the mock-heroic form the relationships of fathers and sons are much more easily identified and resolved than the covert mother-son connection. The comic hero cannot really deal effectively and maturely with a fully experienced, sexually active woman before he resolves a mother-hunger. Kenneth Grahame, author of *The Wind in the Willows*, has observed that a boy's growing up requires an "innate conservatism" that "asks neither poverty nor riches, but only immunity from change." Intimacy with women means both change and challenge.[35] To counteract that psychological dilemma in literary terms, the search for security lies beneath the surface of the mock-heroic mode. In Walker Percy's case, the psychological problem was the death of his mother and, at the difficult adolescent age of sixteen, his inability to mourn her passing successfully. Writing up a case study in the 1940s, Janet Rioch explained how one of her patients (who was Walker Percy) worked through his relationship to a surrogate father (guardian Will Percy) and became ever more resentful of his "real father." Yet the process also involved an increasing withdrawal from her, the analyst. The patient grew certain, as she recounted, "that she was untrustworthy and hostile." She attributed the change of attitude to a resentment of "his weak mother," who, he felt, was untrustworthy.[36]

Not surprisingly, mothers do not figure very prominently in Percy's novels. Binx Bolling's mother Anna is so distant that she might as well not exist. Anna is quite incapable of understanding her first husband John Bolling's chronic depression—his thirty-pound weight loss, interminable walks along the levee, insomnia, and attempts to sleep outside (a mixture of characteristics of Will and Roy Percy). Nor can she grasp her son's need for more than the quizzical detachment she offers, and she considers him yet another chip off the old Bolling block of gloomy introspectives.[37]

Instead of depicting flesh-and-blood mothers, Walker Percy for the most part presented the maternal element in the form of an inanimate object, a cave, as if the womb from which children are born could be detached from its human source. The speculation is less fanciful than at first it may seem. Other novelists have employed the same metaphor and mourned a mother dead too soon or have grieved perpetually for the absence of maternal approval. At once E. M. Forster's Marabar Cave in *A Passage to India* springs to mind. As Wilfred Stone observes, circles, containers, hollows, swellings, caves, and other subterranean sanctuaries are conscious symbols throughout the English novelist's fiction.[38]

Likewise, in Walker Percy an enclosed space often provides the hero safety from a bruising world, but such representations are also sterile, quarantined, exclusionary, and may connote a retreat from life-giving responsibilities. In *The Last Gentleman* the symbolic enclosure is the "young engineer's" subterranean cubicle at Macy's; in *Love in the Ruins*, the motel hideaway; in *Lancelot*, Lance Lamar's pigeonnier, which is itself part of his wife Margot's lavishly perfected but suffocating plantation property, and his cell in the mental institution in New Orleans; in *The Second Coming*, Will Barrett's Lost Cove Cave, which, as Percy plots it, represents the movement toward self-enlightenment out of the darkness of death. Like Dante in *The Divine Comedy*, the middle-aged Will Barrett, in a state of bemusement on the golf course, wanders into a dark wood, and eventually into a cave, but being in the depths helps him to begin his redemption. Commenting on his choice in an interview, Percy remarked, "I like the idea of falling out of a cave, i.e., despair and depression, when [people,] aware of themselves as such, can be[come] closest to life. From cave to greenhouse, courtesy of Sören Kierkegaard and Dr. Jung."[39] Despite the heavy symbolism, the scene of Barrett's falling out of a cave and into the arms of a deranged young woman seems forced, fantastic.

Literary critic Lewis Lawson interprets Percy's use of the cave and its analogy in the setting of the cinema as Percy's philosophical concern for the Platonic ideal, or what he has Binx Bolling call the moment of "certification." "Movie-going," writes Lawson, "unconsciously questing for perfect moments, in other words, guarantees our dissatisfaction with our incarnate lives."[40] Lawson's shrewd observations, however, do not exhaust the possibilities. The womblike structures, mysterious and primal, are the places where myths and dreams are born.[41]

The caves, as well as cavelike movie houses where images flit across a screen and other shadowy spaces, are introduced without much guidance to their inner meaning because Percy himself scarcely wished to signal the origin in an area of his life to which he never referred in any of his scores of interviews. These interiors can be secret and dark, the very core of depression, anonymity, nothingness, and the prospect of death which the writer struggles to deny in the very act of writing. Without paradox or contradiction, it is also the center of religious experience, the monastic communion with God as well. Borrowing perhaps from Carl Jung's theories of the "anima" to be found at the heart of men, Norman Douglas, a novelist and friend of Will Percy, observed that from the earliest of times, caves have represented "the feminine principle," the ancient desire of "mankind to shelter in some Cloven Rock" and find safety in "the sacred womb of Mother Earth who gives us food and receives us after death."[42]

From the caves, so many of the mock heroes, Walker Percy's among their ranks, depart on quests for salvation. One is reminded of the cave on the road that the ambitious peasant Julien Sorel takes to visit his bourgeois friend

Fouqué in Stendhal's *The Red and the Black*.[43] In Percy's *The Second Coming*, the metaphor of a cave is still more emphatically a symbol of maternal security as well as sterility and male renewal, as if, in the language of religious revival, the hero had been born again. Will argues to himself that he must go "to the desert place" (by which he means the cave) and there "wait for God to give a sign. If no sign is forthcoming," he expects the site of rebirth to become his grave, for "there I shall die. But people will know why I died: because there is no sign."[44] Why does it matter that "people" should know or not know? Is it not enough for a hero to comprehend in his own heart? The yearning for the maternal may go unanswered. It leaves the hero in a problematic state, one that continues to the very end of *The Second Coming*, one of his most popular but also most perplexing novels.

Both Stendhal and Percy, who lost their mothers early in their lives, were deeply affected by a code of honor in which fear of ridicule and pursuit of perfection were guiding principles. With regard to the latter aim, Will Percy in 1938 wrote his adoptive son, "I can very well understand how you feel that to be anything less than the greatest in your line would be a failure."[45] Not surprisingly, *The Red and the Black* was one of Walker Percy's favorite novels and one that he reread many times.[46] The writers shared much in common. Both Stendhal and Percy, writing in the mock-heroic mode, longed for escape from the humdrum—"everydayness" in Walker's lexicon—because normal routines and expectations seem to the melancholy sufferer a corrupt and soulless milieu. Stendhal's mother died when her child was seven years old. "With my mother, there ended all the happiness of my childhood," Stendhal grieved. "My psychological life had begun." [47] And both Percy and Stendhal had fathers whose depressive moods cast a somber shadow on the domestic scene just when their sons most needed adult affection and guidance. It is scarcely a wonder that Percy, like Stendhal, created only one mother in his published fiction—Binx Bolling's. Tom More, Will Barrett, and Lance Lamar are motherless.

It is not enough to attribute this peculiarity of orphaned heroes to Percy's repression of his own mother. Southern literature, reflecting a salient feature of regional culture itself, also helps to eliminate such figures or render them in negative terms. Of course, women mattered in Southern life, but their influence was too threatening to the male ego subject to the overly masculine dictates of the regional ethic. Effeminacy was thought to be the horrifying peril into which overly protective mothers placed their sons. In Walker Percy's case, the loose-wristed mannerisms of his Uncle Will, about whom Mississippians have always been ambivalent, were bound to embarrass the young Walker, particularly after he lost his mother in the car accident. He was determined not to be like his cousin in that respect, yet throughout his early years Walker found comfort in the presence of avuncular bachelors like Huger Jervey, one of Will Percy's friends. These men, including Will, served as *both* surrogate fathers and mothers, a point that Rioch would have appreciated if her work with Walker had continued after 1942, when Will Percy died.

The novelist's distant relationship with his mother by no means meant that he could not create believable women in his stories. Yet he did not, as literary critics have often pointed out. Why? One factor is the nature of the mock-heroic itself. Women in the mock-heroic novel are useful as sexual commodities but are secondary to the real problems in the life of the hero. His main task is self-discovery, and making a happy match is only one of the assignments.[48] More important, Percy's own fragile sense of selfhood limited the kind of women with whom he could feel comfortable in literary and perhaps in personal terms. Percy's heroines are sometimes compliant beauty queens like Kitty Vaught in *The Last Gentleman.* Sharon Kincaid, Binx Bolling's secretary with whom he has an affair, belongs in that category, too, although Binx never perceives her as very real. Sharon is instead an abstraction, a symbol of a Kierkegaardian rotation or "the experiencing of the new beyond the expectation of the experiencing of the new.[49] Yet most of the main female characters are childlike replications of the heroes' own depression—the suicidal Kate in *The Moviegoer,* the gang-raped Anna in *Lancelot,* the nearly voiceless Allison in *The Second Coming.* In other words, they are not women in their own right but aspects of Walker's own inner life, projections of himself and his problems of alienation and sense of uncompleted mourning.

Underlining this point even more, as Percy himself grew older he continued to write about men younger than himself, and, still more curiously, men whose most serious love interests are younger still. These are the narcissistic fantasies of the aging American male—sometimes acted upon but just as often remaining harmless daydreams. In fact, Allison Huger in *The Second Coming* is so much younger than the aging Will Barrett that, needing his manly strength and experience, she is as much daughter as lover.[50]

Thus Percy's heroines in most instances are love objects for the heroes, but if they are kinfolk, they matter. Family history helps to explain that literary preference—the exclusivity of the inner circle whereby the first duty was to close ranks during times of stress and assist each other. Kate in *The Moviegoer* and Lucy in his last work, *The Thanatos Syndrome*, are not just lovers of the two heroes, Binx Bolling and Tom More, but their cousins as well: figuratively speaking, they carry the Percy blood. Kate is almost the mirror image of Binx in her own depression, as if male or female cannot escape its effects, which was, as we know, the family tragedy.

If Catherine Warfield and Ellen Lee were imprisoned behind their cultural walls, so too was Walker Percy. With him, as with other white Southern male authors of his and earlier generations, an equality of the sexes simply did not enter the imagination. Whenever an equality was contemplated, however, Percy made clear his region's, and perhaps his own, sense of discomfiture at signs of female aggressiveness. In the only reference to the Percy-related female writers (about whom he knew little or nothing), he noted in *Lancelot* that Jefferson Davis had been "set up in style by another strong-minded woman at Beauvoir." The Victorian lady in question was the brilliant widowed novelist Sarah Dorsey, Percy's cousin, who had befriended, housed, and fed the ex-Confederate leader at her Gulf Coast plantation home from 1877 until her death in 1879.[51]

Moreover, the ideal of male power and female submissiveness had its bearing on the treatment of depression within Percy's novels. Kate Cutrer in *The Moviegoer* and Allie Huger in *The Second Coming*, for instance, are victims of depression just as are their partners Binx Bolling and the aging Will Barrett. Yet the author compels the reader to see them in quite different ways, for reasons that a Renaissance scholar, Juliana Schiesari, has explained.

She points out that melancholia in men is held to be en-
nobling, whereas in women it signifies neurotic weakness,
helplessness.[52] Even Binx is suspicious when Kate appears
suddenly to rejoice in her newfound liberation. She claims
to have achieved her freedom by quitting her analyst. She
exults that when she remained silent in the session she was
not repressing any thoughts, but simply had nothing to say.
"Long ago I learned to be wary of Kate's revelations. These
exalted moments," Binx observes, precede episodes of "the
blackest depression. . . . She will not feel wonderful long."[53]

Despite being close to her in years, Binx Bolling acts
also like a quite appropriate father figure in relationship to
the woman he loves. In *The Second Coming* Will Barrett
is old enough to be Allie's father. In her illness, Allison
is even more childlike than Kate in *The Moviegoer*. Matters, however, are more complicated than such a confusion
of guises might indicate. Though acting his father's role,
Binx has been forced into playing the part by his surrogate
father, Aunt Emily. Uncle Will, upon whom the character
is based, had always insisted on the duty of perpetuating
family honor and assisting those in the clan in need. Thus
in fiction Binx Bolling is expected to care for Kate as an
officer might a wounded soldier under his command. In
fact, Aunt Emily even says at one point that Binx should
"hold the fort" until Sam Yerger, a family friend, can ar-
rive to help out.[54] But carrying out a duty assigned by a
family member is no way to discover who one is, particularly if the duty is to marry a cousin so like oneself. In other
words, we again find that Walker Percy is as restricted in
his imaginative world as his female predecessors had been
in theirs.

Such limitation is evident in the way the novel concludes.

———

Binx serves as the protector and patriarch of his cousin and lover. He will do for her what she cannot do for herself in her illness.[55] By this device, Percy would seem to have provided a most effective closure to the novel, for it suggests how love can be a redemptive force. Yet it is unsatisfactory. Kate and Binx are too alike, two reeds leaning against each other in the wind. Binx has learned much from his experiences in dealing with a woman suffering from deep melancholia, but the reader recognizes that the step toward maturity is not quite so impressive as the author perhaps intended it to be. After all, the illness attributed to Kate is actually the female representation of the male disorder of depression.

The final and concluding point is perhaps the most intriguing of all: the singular interconnection between Walker Percy's greatest novel, *Lancelot,* and its female predecessor, Catherine Ann Warfield's *The Household of Bouverie.* In 1972 Percy wrote Shelby Foote a revealing letter describing how he was planning a novel that would be his crowning achievement if he were not so downcast. Written in the first person, the projected work would concern a middle-aged priest who, while visiting his mother's grave, spies a twenty-year-old girl singing "Bobby McGee" and decides to follow her. The implications were that, imaginatively speaking, Percy was reacting against his own death, against his mother, cold in the ground, and seeking comfort in youthful sexuality. The story in question turned out to be his subsequent novel *Lancelot.* The priest becomes secondary in the final version, and his roguish alter ego, Lance Lamar, becomes the narrator and antihero. He is a murderer and arsonist housed in a narrow cubicle in the

Center for Aberrant Behavior, a high-class institution for the violently insane. Lance is the one, not the priest, to sing the country western song with its gratifying refrain: "*Feeling good was good enough for me / Good enough for me and Bobby McGee.*" Lance is recalling when he was young, lusty, and uncommitted.

Autobiographically, the novel refers back to the time in Percy's own life when Percy had finished his psychiatric therapy and his tubercular convalescence. Yet he was still sorting out the issues that Janet Rioch had helped him to discover. Those problems had included his feelings about his dead mother, father, and guardian, and his tentative efforts to find out who he really was. At this time when "Bobby McGee" was on the Country Hit Parade in 1946, he was pursuing two beautiful women in Sewanee. Although he knew from the start of their prior commitment to other men, he pressed them, one after the other, to marry him.[56] But the Lance the reader encounters in the novel is no youth in search of himself. He has become a bitter melancholic raving against his own self-loathing but seeking some glimmer of spiritual hope to fill the yearning of the child within him for comfort and safety.

The anxieties surrounding the death of mothers are not peculiar to Walker Percy but appear in other Southern literary works. For instance, in the opening scene of Allen Tate's *The Fathers* there occurs a similar episode. Lacy, son of Major John Buchan, who is a depressed and suicidal plantation owner, recalls the day of his mother's funeral. Whether as a deliberate strategy or a matter of inadvertence, Tate has the character fail to mourn her loss. Instead, the author scripts a day on which the son remembers instead that he first began to worship his brother-in-law

George Posey and for the first time began to notice little Jane Posey, to whom he later becomes attached. The scene is almost a perfect representation of the Southern literary paradigm which reflected the patriarchal scheme in regional culture. The subordination of the mother to her youthful and less threatening replacement is the first of these, and the second is the substitution of the male friend for the father. Both proxies help to restore the hero's fragile self-esteem.[57]

At the time he was writing this masterpiece, Percy himself was feeling most dejected. The political events of the Nixon years, the Viet Nam protests, assassinations, and exposures of corruption in high places all contributed to his sense of despair. By his conservative lights, the Catholic Church in which he had first placed his faith in the mid-1940s had lost its way. But worst of all was his own sense of aging, a fear of declining vitality, a return of old paternal ghosts from his troubled past. He was teaching briefly at Louisiana State University in Baton Rouge at the time. A student, stopping by his office, was surprised to hear Percy beckon him in a casual tone, "I guess the central mystery of my life will always be why my father killed himself. Come here, have a seat." [58] The opening lines of *Lancelot* have a similar ring: "Come into my cell. Make yourself at home."

Not long afterward, Percy abruptly left his home in Louisiana for Nevada and hiked into the mountains and its caves. The sudden excursion brings to mind Stendhal's Julien Sorel, who also seeks some special, romantic insight into himself in his dry mountain grotto above Besançon, and returns from the wilderness renewed. Desert dryness was always associated with the humor of black bile. In literary terms during the Renaissance, the accompanying imagery of lifeless, austerely beautiful desert, blackness of night, and abandoned places matched the human condition—analogies that writers like Edgar Allan Poe and other practitioners of the gothic adopted.

In *The Last Gentleman*, also a novel of interlocking honor and despondency, Jamie Vaught's death scene is fittingly played out in the New Mexican desert. Furthermore, Will Percy had chosen that sort of location, the Grand Canyon, for completing *Lanterns on the Levee*, and Walker had lived for a time near Santa Fe.[59] In *Lancelot*, Percy has the hero remark, "Most people will die or exist as the living dead. Everything will go back to the desert." And Lance dreams of being in a room "in an abandoned house in a desert place," with an anonymous woman moving about with an air of possession. A man moves in a different way, but a woman "is at home in a room. The room is an extension of her."[60]

The story line bears an uncanny resemblance to Catherine Ann Warfield's *The Household of Bouverie*. Both novels concern an aristocratic Southern plantation owner suffering from deep depression and unable to experience love but only anger, jealousy, and impotent frustration. When I told Walker Percy that one of his collateral ancestors had written a story about a mad Faustian hero with scientific interests who murdered his wife's lover and spent most of his life self-imprisoned for the crime, he replied with a laugh, "I'd never use a hokey plot like that." The resemblance might be called merely superficial, but that would be an error. Both Warfield's Erastus Bouverie and Walker Percy's Lance Lamar are victims of mania and depression, so much so that they swing between complete nullity and passivity of an androgynous character to violent, compulsive actions as a means not only to prove their own existence but to reassert their power over those near them, particularly their women.

In seeking a final victory over Will Percy's broadsword virtues and coldly antisexual prescriptions, Walker inadvertently chose a genre, protagonist, and plot that had been used by one of his nineteenth-century relatives in her most popular novel. The concept of a Southern plantation owner who is morose, cheerless in character, and largely conscienceless in deed owes something to the surviving family memories of Charles Percy, Warfield's grandfather and Walker Percy's thrice-great grandfather.[61] Both Warfield and Walker Percy explicitly use Charles Percy's gothic image in fashioning their portrait of a mad patriarchal figure.[62] Their fury against rival men and their misogyny suggest a Jungian resentment of their own "feminine" natures, an androgyny that is hidden behind their basic hostility toward women. Like Erastus Bouverie, Lance Lamar cannot endure feminine independence of spirit which threatens his brittle sense of himself as a man.

The Household of Bouverie and *Lancelot* also make use of the gothic scientific paraphernalia not only because those conventions lend themselves to subjective explorations of character but because the family illness, being genetic in character, would naturally be involved in such realms of science fiction as medicine, electronics, and the pseudo-science of alchemy. The Gothic form lends itself particularly to the prospect of genetic madness, about which both Percy and his female precursor were acutely aware. Edgar Allan Poe, to whom both writers were indebted in employing this genre about familial tragedy, set the precedent. He has Roderick Usher, the protagonist in *The Fall of the*

House of Usher, remark that his own "nervous agitation," which oscillated between the "vicious and sullen," was "a constitutional and a family evil" for which no remedy, no relief could ever be found.[63] Scientific fantasies and inventions to overcome the horrors of such diseases of the mind fill many pages of gothic tales. Both Lance Lamar and Erastus Bouverie inhabit a private world in which scientific experimentation is separated from human dimensions— Lance in the pigeonnier at Belle Isle, his plantation home— and Erastus in the second-floor chambers and cupola of Bouverie, cut off from any visible access because he must be hidden from the authorities for the murder of Luther Quintilian, Camilla's second husband.

Belle Isle and Bouverie's house, in their antiquity, vulnerability to fire, and large proportions represent the honor-conscious, oversized egos of their proud, melancholic owners. Likewise, they are situated in isolation from ordinary society. Bouverie's house, with its hideaway in the upper story, is emblematic of the schizophrenic marriage that the unhappy Camilla must endure with a manic husband. Just as Bouverie experiments with batteries and elixirs to perpetuate youth, Walker Percy's Lance Lamar utilizes the new technology of a blood test to prove the illegitimacy of his daughter Siobhan and infra-red video equipment to detect the shadowy signs of his wife Margot's lovemaking. With regard to the antihero's electrical interests, one is reminded that in Walker Percy's *Love in the Ruins* Dr. Thomas More, the experimental psychiatrist, invents a lapsometer, an electronic machine similar to Bouverie's galvanic battery and likewise applied to the head.

Both instruments are used to alter the mental states of the victims. Whereas Bouverie makes no large claims for the healing powers of his galvanic battery, More's lapsometer is supposed to remove inhibitions, suicidal temptations, and fears—remedies which in the wrong hands could transform human personality for the worse. In Percy's satirical imagination, such tinkering with the psyche is modern social engineering gone awry. In Warfield's hands, science itself is not seen in such philosophical or ethical terms but rather represents in its odd childishness how the mania of a patriarch in whom resides all power could destroy love and marriage.

Both *Lancelot* and *The Household of Bouverie* employ the concept of the Holy Grail, which in Warfield's work appears as her hero's elixir of gold that promises the salvation of perpetual youth rather than holy grace. The legend was always associated with alchemy and the primitive understanding of Christianity in northwestern European cultures.[64] Quite ingeniously, Percy turns the myth upside down, so that Lance informs Father John that he, Lance, seeks not a Holy Grail, but rather an "Unholy" one: the source of evil instead of salvation. Warfield also perceived the blasphemy of man's assumption of God's powers and identified that repudiation with her agnostic father, with the irreligious Charles Percy, perhaps with an unchristianized patriarchy itself.

On a very visible level Walker Percy's creation of Lance Lamar involved a reaction to those terrible losses that the Percy family had endured—the snatching away of parents and normal expectations by the violence of sudden death, and more subtly by their replacement with an exotic tradition that stimulated the mind but taught too little of joy and certainty. The world is unjust! Walker Percy's heroes would like to cry out. But instead, the shout dies in the throat, memory fails, passion shrivels to a twitch of the knee, a tic in the face. Or, as in Lance's case, the repressed outrage might find expression in revenge, as if the act could restore a sense of belonging.

Yet for all the negative aspects of the Percy family saga, what a story its members could tell and often did. The Percys represent the best and also the uniqueness of the Southern white experience. Some of them were able to write about it with great or modest success, but their contribution in either event may serve as an inspiration for a family beset with the curse of melancholia and yet blessed with its accompanying gift of creativity. As Walker Percy proclaimed in *The Second Coming*, "Death in none of its guises shall prevail over me, because I know all the names of death." That spirit, born of pain, had also guided his cousin Will and the Percy writers of the nineteenth century.[65]

NOTES

Preface

1. Lucinda H. MacKethan, *Daughters of Time: Creating Woman's Voice in Southern Story* (Athens: University of Georgia Press, 1990), 1–3.

One. *The First Percy Writers*

1. Mrs. Catharine [*sic*] Warfield and Mrs. Eleanor Percy Lee, The Two Sisters of the West, *The Wife of Leon, and Other Poems* (1843; Cincinnati: E. Morgan, 1845); Mrs. Catherine Ann Warfield and Mrs. Eleanor Percy Lee, *The Indian Chamber, and Other Poems* (New York: private printing, 1846); Catherine Ann Warfield [A Southern Lady], *The Household of Bouverie, Or, the Elixir of Gold* (2 vols.; New York: Derby & Jackson, 1860); *The Romance of the Green Seal* (New York: Beadle, 1866); *The Romance of Beauseincourt: An Episode Extracted from the Retrospect of Miriam Monfort* (New York: G. W. Carleton, 1867); *Miriam Monfort* (New York: D. Appleton, 1873); *Hester Howard's Temptation* (Philadelphia: J. B. Peterson, 1875); *A Double Wedding, Or, How She Was Won* (Philadelphia: T. B. Peterson, 1875); *Lady Ernestine, Or, the Absent Lord of Rocheforte* (Philadelphia: T. B. Peterson, 1876);

Ferne Fleming (Philadelphia: T. B. Peterson, 1877); *The Cardinal's Daughter* (New York: T. B. Peterson, 1877). Sarah A. Dorsey, *Recollections of Henry Watkins Allen, Brigadier-General Confederate States Army, Ex-Governor of Louisisna* (New York: M. Doolady, 1866); Sarah A. Dorsey [Filia], *Agnes Graham: A Novel* (Philadelphia: Claxton, Remsen and Haffelfinger, 1869); Sarah A. Dorsey [Filia], *Athalie, or A Southern Villeggiatura: 'A Winter's Tale'* (Philadelphia: Claxton, Remsen, Haffelfinger, 1872); Sarah A. Dorsey [Filia], *Lucia Dare: A Novel* (New York: M. Doolady, 1867); Sarah A. Dorsey, *Panola: A Tale of Louisiana* (Philadelphia: T. B. Peterson, 1877); Kate Lee Ferguson, *Cliquot: A Racing Story of Ideal Beauty* (Philadelphia: T. B. Peterson, 1889).

2. Joel Williamson, *William Faulkner and Southern History* (New York: Oxford University Press, 1993). Lawrence J. Friedman is the author of *Menninger: The Family and the Clinic* (New York: Alfred A. Knopf, 1990).

3. See Anne Stevenson, *Bitter Fame: A Life of Sylvia Plath* (Boston: Houghton Mifflin, 1989); Linda W. Wagner-Martin, *Sylvia Plath: A Biography* (New York: Simon & Schuster, 1987); Diane Wood Middlebrook, *Anne Sexton: A Biography* (Boston: Houghton Mifflin, 1991).

4. Quotations in Helen Taylor, *Gender, Race, and Region in the Writings of Grace King, Ruth McEnery Stuart, and Kate Chopin* (Baton Rouge: Louisiana State University Press, 1989), 24.

5. Anne Goodwyn Jones, *Tomorrow Is Another Day: The Woman Writer in the South, 1859–1936* (Baton Rouge: Louisiana State University Press, 1981), 9.

6. Sarah Ellis Dorsey to Lyulph Stanley, January 3, 1872, #1094, Stanley Family MSS, John Rylands Library, University of Manchester, Manchester, England.

7. Quoted in Joanna Russ, *How to Suppress Women's Writing* (Austin: University of Texas Press, 1983), 11.

8. Ibid., 95, 97.

9. Ibid., 42–43.

10. See Bertram Wyatt-Brown, *The House of Percy* (New York: Oxford University Press, 1994), chapters 6–8.

11. See John Hereford Percy, *The Percy Family of Mississippi and Louisiana* (Baton Rouge: Claitor, 1943), 1–2; William Alexander Percy, *Lanterns on the Levee: Recollections of a Planter's Son* (1941; Baton Rouge: Louisiana State University Press, 1973), 39–40; Wyatt-Brown, *The House of Percy*, chapter 1.

12. William B. Hamilton and William D. McCain, "Wealth in the Natchez Region: Inventories of the Estate of Charles Percy, 1794 and 1804," *Journal of Mississippi History* 10 (October 1948):280–303.

13. Terry Alford, *Prince among Slaves* (New York: Harcourt Brace Jovanovich, 1977), 112–13; John C. Calhoun to James Monroe, April 17, 1815 (quotation), David Holmes to President James Madison, January 19, 1813, Microfilm 438, Roll no. 8, 10-19-3, Territorial Papers, National Archives, Washington; Josiah Simpson to Secretary of State, March 28, 1815, Appointment Office Files, Department of State, National Archives, Washington; *Biographical and Historical Memoirs of Mississippi* (2 vols.; Chicago: Goodspeed, 1891), 1:733; William Diamond, "Nathaniel A. Ware, National Economist," *Journal of Southern History* 5 (November 1939):501–26; Broadus Mitchell, "Nathaniel A. Ware," in *Dictionary of American Biography* (20 vols.; New York: Charles Scribner's Sons, 1928–37), 19:451.

14. Phyllis Greenacre, "The Family Romance of the Artist," in *The Psychoanalytic Study of the Child, Vol. XIII* (New York: International Universities Press, 1958), 9–36; Felix Brown, "Bereavement and Lack of a Parent in Childhood," in E. Miller, ed., *Foundations of Child Psychiatry* (London: Pergamon, 1968), 435–55; George H. Pollock, "The Mourning Process and Creative Organizational Change," *Journal of the American Psychoanalytic Association* 45 (No. 1, 1977):3–34; Frederick K. Goodwin and Kay Redfield Jamison, *Manic-Depressive Illness* (New York: Oxford University Press, 1990), 332–67.

15. Quotation, Mary Tardy [Ida Raymond], *The Living Female Writers of the South* (Philadelphia: Claxton, Remsen and Haffelfinger, 1872), 18. On Ware's Southwestern property ventures, see Catherine Ann Warfield to John L. Darragh, October 23, November 3, 1853, June 17, 1854, April 3, 1855, May 2, 1855; Nathaniel Ware Warfield to Darragh, October 16, 1853, including inventory of the Estate of N. A. Ware, January 5, 1854, John L. Darragh, demurrer, document 27-0106, dated March 1, 1854, and settlement, March 29, 1854 (document 27-0108), John L. Darragh MSS, Rosenberg Library, Galveston, Texas. The clerk's office in the courthouse in Galveston has records of Ware's purchases beginning in 1842.

16. Mary Tardy [Ida Raymond], *Southland Writers: Biographical and Critical Sketches of the Living Female Writers of the South* (Philadelphia: Claxton, Remsen & Haffelfinger, 1870), 2:28.

17. Tardy, *Southland Writers*, 2:30; also Tardy, *Living Female Writers*, 18.

18. Tardy, *Southland Writers*, 2:30.

19. See, for similar cases, the Brontë sisters and Constance Woolson, an American writer and friend of Henry James: Sandra Gilbert and Susan Gubar, *The Madwoman in the Attic: The Woman Writer and the Nineteenth-Century Literary Imagination* (New Haven: Yale University Press, 1979); Joan Myers Weimer, ed., *Women Artists, Women Exiles: 'Miss Grief' and Other Stories by Constance Fenimore Woolson* (New Brunswick, N.J.: Rutgers University Press, 1988), x–xi.

20. Tardy, *Living Female Writers*, 21–22.

21. Eleanor Percy Ware, "To ———," Philadelphia, 1830, Poetry Notebook, 1830–1837, and Commonplace Book, Ware Family Papers, Louisiana and Lower Mississippi Valley Collections, Hill Memorial Library, Louisiana State University, Baton Rouge.

20. John Seely Hart, *A Manual of American Literature* (1873; Johnson Reprint Co., 1969), 507.

23. See Eleanor Percy Lee to Catherine Ann Warfield, June 22, 1843, May 10, 1844 (quotation), July 8, 1849, Ware Papers.

24. Warfield and Lee, *The Wife of Leon*, i.

25. Mark Twain, *The Adventures of Huckleberry Finn*, ed. Henry Nash Smith (Boston: Houghton Mifflin, n.d.), 87–88.

26. See Julia Deane Freeman [Mary Forrest], *Women of the South Distinguished in Literature* (New York: Derby & Jackson, 1861), 151–57, for poems of a derivative character.

27. Quoted in Frank L. Mott, *Golden Multitudes* (New York, 1947), 122.

28. See Mary Kelley, "The Literary Domestics: Private Women on a Public Stage," in Hamilton Cravens, ed., *Ideas in America's Cultures from Republic to Mass Society* (Ames, Iowa: Iowa State University Press, 1982), 84.

29. James Wood Davidson, *Living Writers of the South* (New York: Carleton, 1869), 600–602; "I Have Seen This Place Before," in Warfield and Lee, *The Wife of Leon*, 232.

30. Warfield and Lee, *The Indian Chamber*, 29.

31. "The Natchez Lighthouse," in ibid., 42–44; "A Tale of Life," in ibid., 243–44; Eleanor Percy Lee, Commonplace Book, Ware Papers.

32. [Catherine Ann Warfield] to Catherine Lee Ferguson, n.d., Commonplace Book, Ware Papers; Freeman, *Women of the South Distinguished in Literature*, 151.

33. Warfield and Lee, *The Indian Chamber*, 191.

34. "They Tell Me There's an Eastern Bird," in ibid., 105; Nathaniel A. Ware, *Henry Belden* (Cincinnati: private printing, 1848).

35. See Eleanor Percy Ware, Commonplace Book, 9, Ware Papers. See also in a similar vein "The Wanderer," in Warfield and Lee, *The Wife of Leon*, 94–97.

36. "Remorse," in Warfield and Lee, *The Indian Chamber*, 69.

37. Ibid., 65–73.

38. "My Cousin Jane," in ibid., 262.

39. Tardy, *Southland Writers*, 2:38.

40. Ibid.

41. Eleanor Percy Lee to Catherine Ann Warfield, May 10, 1844, Ware Papers.

42. Lee to Warfield, May 10, 1844, Ware Papers.

43. Russ, *How to Suppress Women's Writing*, 50.

44. Eleanor Percy Lee to William Henry Lee, July 8, 1849, Ware Papers.

45. Tardy, *Southland Writers*, 2:31.

46. Ibid., 2:27.

47. Davidson, *Living Writers of the South*, 600.

48. Catherine Sinclair, *Jane Bouverie, Or, Prosperity and Adversity* (New York: Harper & Brothers, 1851); Warfield, *The Household of Bouverie.*

49. See Anne Lewis Hardeman Journals, entry for June 3, 1866, in Michael O'Brien, ed., *An Evening When Alone: Four Journals of Single Women in the South, 1827–1867* (Charlottesville: University Press of Virginia, 1993), 379.

50. Freeman, *Women of the South Distinguished in Literature,* 117; Davidson, *Living Writers of the South,* 603; Jane Tompkins, *Sensational Designs: The Cultural Work of American Fiction, 1790–1860* (New York: Oxford University Press, 1985), xii, 4–5, 27–35. Tompkins's comments on the nature of Hawthorne's contemporary reputation make a comparison with Warfield less astonishing.

51. Elizabeth Moss, *Domestic Novels in the Old South: Defenders of Southern Culture* (Baton Rouge: Louisiana State University Press, 1992); Mary Ann Wimsatt, "Antebellum Fiction," in Louis D. Rubin, Jr., et al., eds., *The Literary History of the South* (Baton Rouge: Louisiana State University Press, 1985), 92–107; Ritchie D. Watson, Jr., *The Cavalier in Virginia Fiction* (Baton Rouge: Louisiana State University Press, 1985).

52. Tardy, *Southland Writers*, 1:205; Ralph A. Wooster, *The Secession Conventions of the South* (Princeton: Princeton Uni-

versity Press, 1962), 108; Sarah Dorsey resolution of January 23 in New Orleans *Times-Picayune*, January 29, 1861; Tardy, *Living Female Writers*, 22; Lewis Baker, *The Percys of Mississippi: Politics and Literature in the New South* (Baton Rouge: Louisiana State University Press, 1983), 5–6.

53. See Tompkins, *Sensational Designs*.

54. Quotations from Tardy, *Living Female Writers*, 22.

55. Henry James, quoted in Henry Nash Smith, "The Scribbling Women and the Cosmic Success Story," *Critical Inquiry* 1 (September 1974), 50.

56. See Charlotte Brontë, *Jane Eyre* (1847; London: Penguin, 1966).

57. Brontë, *Jane Eyre*, 242.

58. Quoted in Q. D. Leavis introduction, ibid., 7–8.

59. Warfield, *The Household of Bouverie*, 2:7.

60. Quotation from Lucy M. Freibert, review of Susan Warner, *The Wide, Wide World* (1850; New York: Feminist Press, 1987), in *Legacy* 4 (Fall 1987):67.

61. A friend of Charlotte Brontë quoted in Leavis introduction, *Jane Eyre*, 7–8.

62. Catherine Ann Warfield, undated MSS Poem, "Written for Mrs Stephens' Magazine," Cincinnati Historical Society, Cincinnati, Ohio.

63. Tardy, *Living Female Writers*, 26.

64. Ibid., 23, 25, 27.

65. Warfield, *Miriam Monfort*, 241–42; Norman N. Holland, *The I* (New Haven: Yale University Press, 1985), 35; Holland, "Literary Interpretation and Three Phases of Psychoanalysis," in Alan Roland, ed., *Psychoanalysis, Creativity, and Literature: A French-American Inquiry* (New York: Columbia University Press, 1978), 233–47; and Alan Roland, "Toward a Reorientation of Psychoanalytic Literary Criticism," in Roland, *Psychoanalysis, Creativity and Literature*, 254–58 (quotation, 257).

66. Tardy, *Living Female Writers*, 25–26.

---

67. Lucinda H. MacKethan, *Daughters of Time: Creating Woman's Voice in Southern Story* (Athens: University of Georgia Press, 1990), 4.

Two. *Kate Ferguson, Scandal, and Percy Mythmaking*

1. See front matter, Kate Lee Ferguson, *Cliquot: A Racing Story of Ideal Beauty* (Philadelphia: T. B. Peterson, 1889); Wayne Mixon, "'A Great Pure Fire': Sexual Passion in the Virginia Fiction of Amélie Rives," in Winfred B. Moore, Jr., and Joseph F. Tripp, eds., *Looking South: Chapters in the Story of an American Region* (Westport, Conn.: Greenwood Press, 1989), 207–16.

2. Mixon, "'A Great, Pure Fire,'" 207–16, quotation 210.

3. Michael O'Brien, *The Idea of the American South, 1920–1941* (Baltimore: Johns Hopkins University Press, 1979), 11.

4. William Alexander Percy, *Lanterns on the Levee: Recollections of a Planter's Son* (1941; Baton Rouge: Louisiana State University Press, 1973), 70.

5. William F. Holmes, "William Alexander Percy and the Bourbon Era in the Yazoo-Mississippi Delta," *Mississippi Quarterly* 26 (Winter 1972–73), 71–87, especially 75–76; James Cobb, *The Most Southern Place on Earth: The Mississippi Delta* (New York: Oxford University Press, 1992), 128; Robert L. Brandfon, *Cotton Kingdom of the New South: A History of the Yazoo Mississippi Delta from Reconstruction to the Twentieth Century* (Cambridge, Mass.: Harvard University Press, 1967), 150.

6. C. Vann Woodward, *Origins of the New South, 1877–1913* (Baton Rouge: Louisiana State University Press, 1951), 66–74.

7. See Georgia Payne Durham Pinkston, *A Place to Remember: East Carroll Parish, Louisiana, 1832–1976* (Baton Rouge: Claitor, 1977), 237–39; Last Will and Testament of Pickens Compton, February 23, 1867, Will Book 1, 379, Washington County Courthouse, Greenville, Miss.

---

8. Entry for December 23, 1904, Henry Waring Ball Diary, 57, Mississippi Department of Archives and History. Other copies are located at the Southern Historical Collection (microfilm), Wilson Library, University of North Carolina, Chapel Hill, and the William Alexander Percy Memorial Library, Greenville, Miss. (photocopy).

9. Entry for December 23, 1904, Ball Diary.

10. Entry for August 9, 1904, Ball Diary.

11. Entry for May 1, 1886, Ball Diary.

12. Entry for January 1, 1888, Ball Diary.

13. Percy, *Lanterns on the Levee*, 70.

14. Weiss and Goldstein, which had underwritten the General, had gone bankrupt and the bond had not been renewed with another firm. See Greenville *Times*, July 14, 28, 1894.

15. Percy, *Lanterns on the Levee*, 68; Greenville *Times*, July 14, 21, 1894.

16. Greenville *Times*, July 14, August 11, 1894; William F. Holmes, "William Alexander Percy and the Bourbon Era in the Yazoo-Mississippi Delta," *Mississippi Quarterly* 26 (Winter 1972): 71–88.

17. *Biographical and Historical Memoirs of Mississippi* (Chicago: Goodspeed, 1891), 1:738.

18. Greenville *Times*, August 18, 1894.

19. Ibid.

20. *Biographical and Historical Memoirs of Mississippi* 1:713. Also see Ferguson, "Life in the Confederate States Army, July, 1864–May, 1865," folder 7, and folder 24 ("Fiesta of Corpus Christi in the Andes Mountains," at Tambillo, Ecuador), Samuel Wragg Ferguson Papers, Louisiana and Lower Mississippi Valley Collections, Hill Memorial Library, Louisiana State University, Baton Rouge.

21. Percy, *Lanterns on the Levee*, 71–72.

22. Ibid., 72, 73 (quotation).

---

23. Claude Lévi-Strauss, *Structural Anthropology*, trans. Claire Jacobson and Brooke Grundfest Schoepf (New York: Basic Books, 1963), 229.

24. Percy, *Lanterns on the Levee*, 72.

25. Ibid., 74.

26. Ibid., 74–75.

27. William Alexander Percy to Gerstle Mack, December 27, 1939, copy, from the files of Jay Tolson, kindly lent.

Three. *"Desperate Storytelling"*

1. Virginia Woolf, "On Being Ill," in *The Moment and Other Essays* (1948; New York: Harcourt Brace Jovanovich, 1974), 10.

2. Foote quoted in Jay Tolson, *Pilgrim in the Ruins: A Life of Walker Percy* (New York: Simon & Schuster, 1992), 256.

3. Robert Coles, *Walker Percy: An American Search* (Boston: Little, Brown, 1978), 62–63.

4. Robert Cubbage, "A Visitor Interview: Novelist Walker Percy," in Lewis A. Lawson and Victor A. Kramer, eds., *More Conversations with Walker Percy* (Jackson, Miss.: University Press of Mississippi, 1993), 187.

5. Phil McCombs, "Century of Thanatos: Walker Percy and His Subversive Message," in Lawson and Kramer, *More Conversations with Walker Percy*, 198.

6. Walker Percy, "From Facts to Fiction," in Walker Percy, *Signposts in a Strange Land*, ed. Patrick Samway (New York: Farrar, Giroux and Straus, 1991), 189–90.

7. See Tolson, *Pilgrim in the Ruins*, 83.

8. Charles T. Bunting, "An Afternoon with Walker Percy," in Lewis A. Lawson and Victor A. Kramer, eds., *Conversations with Walker Percy* (Jackson, Miss.: University Press of Mississippi, 1985), 44.

9. Tolson, *Pilgrim in the Ruins*, 279. For an eloquent examination of the relationship of art and melancholy, see Kay Redfield

Jamison, *Touched by Fire: Manic-Depressive Illness and the Artistic Temperament* (New York: Basic Books, 1993, especially 102–47.

10. Albert Rothenberg, *Creativity and Madness: New Findings and Old Stereotypes* (Baltimore: Johns Hopkins University Press, 1990), 47 (quotation), and "Creativity, Articulation, and Psychotherapy," *Journal of the American Academy of Psychoanalysis* 11 (1983):55–84; Arthur Koestler, *The Act of Creation* (1964; New York: Dell, 1975), 316–17; Jamison, *Touched by Fire*, 117.

11. Walker Percy to Shelby Foote, May 12, 1960, Walker Percy MSS, Southern Historical Collection, University of North Carolina, Chapel Hill.

12. Natalie Angier, "An Old Idea about Genius Wins New Scientific Support," New York *Times*, October 12, 1993, B-5; Marshall W. Alcorn, Jr., and Mark Bracher, "Literature, Psychoanalysis, and the Reformation of the Self: A New Direction for Reader-Response Theory," *PMLA* 100 (May 1985):342–54; Nancy C. Andreasen, "Creativity and Mental Illness: Prevalence Rates in Writers and Their First-Degree Relatives," *American Journal of Psychiatry* 144 (1987):1288–92; N. J. C. Andreasen and A. Cantor, "The Creative Writer: Psychiatric Symptoms and Family History," *Comparative Psychiatry* 15 (1974):123–31; and Frederick K. Goodwin and Kay Redfield Jamison, *Manic-Depressive Illness* (New York: Oxford University Press, 1990), 332–67.

13. Angier, "An Old Idea," B-5.

14. Entry for April 3, 1932, Ball Diary; Greenville *Delta Democrat-Times*, April 2, 1932.

15. Walker Percy, "Introduction," in William Alexander Percy, *Lanterns on the Levee: Recollections of a Planter's Son* (1941; Baton Rouge: Louisiana State University Press, 1973), viii, x, xi; John Griffin Jones, in Lawson and Kramer, *Conversations with Walker Percy*, 258; David L. Cohn, "Eighteenth-Century Chevalier," *Virginia Quarterly Review* 31 (Autumn 1955):562–63.

16. Tolson, *Pilgrim in the Ruins*, 134, 162–78, quotation, 178.

17. Roger B. Salomon, *Desperate Storytelling: Post-Romantic*

Elaborations of the Mock-Heroic Mode (Athens: University of Georgia Press, 1987).

18. Percy, *Lanterns on the Levee*, 223.

19. Willa Cather, *One of Our Own* (1922; Random House, 1991), 370.

20. Walker Percy, *The Moviegoer* (1961; New York: Farrar, Straus, and Giroux, 1973), 25.

21. Ibid., 26–27.

22. Martin Luschei, "*The Moviegoer* as Dissolve," in Panthea Reid Broughton, ed., *The Art of Walker Percy* (Baton Rouge: Louisiana State University Press, 1979), 29.

23. See Ralph C. Wood, *The Comedy of Redemption: Christian Faith and Comic Vision in Four American Novelists* (Notre Dame: University of Notre Dame Press, 1988), 155.

24. Walker Percy, *The Moviegoer*, 55, 200. See Christopher Bollas, "Extractive Introjection," an illuminating unpublished paper presented to the Group for Applied Psychoanalysis, February 19, 1987, University of Florida, Gainesville.

25. Salomon, *Desperate Storytelling*, 35, 43.

26. See, for instance, Lewis A. Lawson, *Following Percy: Essays on Walker Percy's Work* (Troy, N.Y.: Whiston Publishing Co., 1988), 1, 24.

27. Walker Percy, *The Moviegoer*, 25.

28. Ibid., 224.

29. Walker Percy, *The Last Gentleman* (New York: New American Library, 1968), 211 (Union monument).

30. Ibid., 117–18.

31. Ibid., 253–54.

32. Ibid., 258–59.

33. Jo Gullege, "The Reentry Option: An Interview with Walker Percy," in Lawson and Kramer, *Conversations with Walker Percy*, 300.

34. See John T. Irwin, *Doubling and Incest/ Repetition and*

Revenge: A Speculative Reading of Faulkner (Baltimore: Johns Hopkins University Press, 1975), 68–69, 110–11 (quotation from *The Sound and Fury*).

35. Kenneth Grahame, quoted in Salomon, *Desperate Storytelling*, 73.

36. Janet MacKenzie Rioch, "The Transference Phenomenon in Psychoanalytic Therapy," *Psychiatry* 6 (May 1943):152.

37. See Audrey Lots Ladoff, "Love in Walker Percy: A Flight from Ancestry," M.A. thesis, Florida Atlantic University, 1984, pp. 28–29; Walker Percy, *The Moviegoer*, 137–38, 149, 152–53.

38. See E. M. Forster, *A Passage to India* (1924; London: Everyman's Library, 1968), Part 2, Caves, 105–246; Wilfred Stone, *The Cave and the Mountain: A Study of E. M. Forster* (Stanford, Calif.: Stanford University Press, 1966), 298–346.

39. Zoltán Abádi-Nagy, "The Art of Fiction XCVII: Walker Percy," in Lawson and Kramer, *More Conversations with Walker Percy*, 147.

40. Lawson, "Walker Percy's *The Moviegoer:* The Cinema as Cave," in *Following Percy*, 94.

41. Walker Percy, *The Moviegoer*, 216. I am indebted here to Lewis A. Lawson, "Walker Percy's *The Moviegoer:* The Cinema as Cave," *Southern Studies* 29 (Winter 1980):331–54, especially 345–46 and 346n29. See also Lawson, *Following Percy*, 11.

42. Norman Douglas, *Old Calabria* (London: Harmondsworth, 1962), 37.

43. Stendhal, *The Red and the Black*, ed. and trans. Robert N. Adams (1830; New York: W. W. Norton, 1969), 55.

44. Walker Percy, *The Second Coming* (New York: Farrar, Straus, and Giroux, 1980), 193.

45. William Alexander Percy to Walker Percy, May 4, 1938, quoted in Billups Phinizy Spalding, "William Alexander Percy: His Philosophy of Life as Reflected in His Poetry," M.A. thesis, University of Georgia, 1957, 108.

46. Phone conversation with Linda Hobson, November 19, 1993. Dr. Hobson had many conversations with Percy on literary topics and recalls that Stendhal figured in a number of them.

47. Quoted by Joanna Richardson, *Stendhal* (London: Victor Gollancz, 1974), 16 and 17. The quotations come from different sources.

48. Zoltán Abádi-Nagy, interview, 1973, Lawson and Kramer, *Conversations with Walker Percy*, 81.

49. Walker Percy, *The Moviegoer*, 144.

50. See Bertram Wyatt-Brown, "Walker Percy: Autobiographical Fiction and the Aging Process," *Journal of Gerontological Studies* 3 (January 1989): 81–89.

51. See Wyatt-Brown, *The House of Percy*, chapter 8.

52. Juliana Schiesari, *The Gendering of Melancholia: Feminism, Psychoanalysis, and the Symbolics of Loss in Renaissance Literature* (Ithaca: Cornell University Press, 1992).

53. Walker Percy, *The Moviegoer*, 112–13, 114.

54. Ibid., 29.

55. See Adam Phillips, *Winnicott* (Cambridge, Mass.: Harvard University Press, 1988), 11–12; D. W. Winnicott, *The Family and Individual Development* (London: Tavistock Publications, 1965), 18–20.

56. Walker Percy to Shelby Foote, July 4, 1973, Percy MSS, Southern Historical Collection; Tolson, *Pilgrim in the Ruins*, 187–90, 383.

57. Allen Tate, *The Fathers* (New York: G. P. Putnam's Sons, 1938), chapter 1.

58. Tolson, *Pilgrim in the Ruins*, 396.

59. See Lewis Baker, *The Percys of Mississippi: Politics and Literature in the New South* (Baton Rouge: Louisiana State University Press, 1983), 169; Coles, *Walker Percy*, 112.

60. John W. Draper, *The Humors and Shakespeare's Characters* (New York: AMS Press, 1965), 62–80. Laurentius pointed out that "there are many sorts of melancholie: there is one that

is altogether grosse and earthie, cold, and drie: there is another that is hot and adust, men call *atribilis*. . . . The first sort which is grosse and earthie, maketh men altogether slacke in all their actions both of bodie and minde, fearfull, sluggish, and without understanding." (70). Walker Percy, *Lancelot* (New York: Farrar, Straus and Giroux, 1977), 36. See also p. 158.

61. Documents quoted in May Wilson McBee, comp., *Natchez Court Records, 1767–1805: Abstracts of Early Records* (Baltimore: Genealogical Publishing Co., 1979), 98–99, 111; Robert Dow to Robert Percy, February 12, 1794, in John Hereford Percy, *The Percy Family of Mississippi and Louisiana, 1776–1943* (Baton Rouge: Claitor, 1943), 50; Francisco Pousset to Don Manuel Gayoso de Lemos, January 31, 1794, Spanish Records, vol. 28, Book C, p. 95, Spanish Records, Clerk of the Chancery Court, Adams County Courthouse, Natchez, Mississippi, and entry for February 16, 1795, in McBee, *Natchez Court Records*, 111; Daniel Clark to Gayoso, June 11, 1794, Charles Percy, subject file, Mississippi State Department of Archives and History, Jackson.

62. For further use of Charles Percy, see also Walker Percy, *The Thanatos Syndrome* (New York: Farrar, Straus and Giroux, 1987), 136; James Hillman, *Anima: An Anatomy of a Personified Notion* (Dallas: Spring Publications, 1985); William Patrick Day, *In the Circles of Fear and Desire: A Study of Gothic Fantasy* (Chicago: University of Chicago Press, 1985), 23.

63. Poe, quoted in Jamison, *Touched by Fire*, 193.

64. Emma Jung and Marie-Louise von Franz, *The Grail Legend*, trans. Andrea Dykes (1970; New York: Sigo Press, 1986).

65. Percy, *The Second Coming*, 314.

INDEX